In her book, *Peter the Pebble...Peter the Rock*, Dr. Candi MacAlpine has captured the journey of Peter from his beginnings as a new disciple of Yeshua (Jesus) the Messiah to his foundational position as an apostle upon whom Yeshua could and would build the emerging kingdom of Yahweh (God).

His process of transformation chronicled in these pages is applicable to every human. We all have struggles and victories common to Peter and to mankind.

In her authenticity Candi has a unique gift that enables her to be an encouragement to others. With her candid shared experiences and her wisdom learned from her own spiritual journey with Messiah, her book is truly transformative in nature.

—REV. QAUMANIQ SUUQIINA, C.E.A.P.
DR. IGLAHLIQ SUUQIINA
DIRECTORS, INDIGENOUS MESSENGERS INTL.

Your book is such a great and critical message for today, and the chronological take on Peter helps people grab the process of movement and growth so they can see the progress of what destiny looks like for them.

—GARY GOODELL
FOUNDER, THIRD DAY CHURCHES

Dr. Candi MacAlpine has done a wonderful job in illustrating how you and I are to spiritually advance through our spiritual journey of becoming the people we were created to be in the kingdom of God. Walking through the spiritual journey of Peter, she will draw you into your own personal experiences to empower you to recognize where you are in your walk while at the same time pressing you toward the goal of kingdom destiny. I don't know about you as the reader, but I surely can relate to Peter and his journey. In this book, Candi has done a great job of mapping our kingdom growth and maturity through Peter's experiences and calling. I know Candi as a personal friend and colleague. She is the real deal and exudes the love and anointing of Jesus in all aspects of her life and calling. If you desire to journey deeper with your heavenly Father and to become the son or daughter, His kingdom representative that He has destined you be, I highly recommend, *Peter the Pebble...Peter the Rock*, as a must read.

—Rebecca Greenwood
President, Christian Harvest International
Author, *Authority to Tread, Breaking the Bonds of Evil, Destined to Rule* and *Let Our Children Go*

Dr. Candi MacAlpine is an apostolic bridge builder of the twenty-first century. Her new book, *Peter the Pebble...Peter the Rock*, is a prophetic revelation of the process of destiny transformation. With an anecdotal twist to the difficult realities of life experiences, Candi is able to draw you into desiring to walk through, with the Lord, a pebble to rock experience. If you want to be an individual of impact in the world today, this book will help prepare you for how to keep a right heart and perspective as difficulties and challenges come against you. Just like Peter, you also can experience a life changing transformation. Great job Candi, in bring forth a book to equip saints to fulfill destiny and build the church today.

—GALE SHEEHAN
CIAN DIRECTOR (CHRISTIAN INTERNATIONAL
APOSTOLIC NETWORK)

From pebble to rock: the journey. That's what this book could be called. Candi MacAlpine wrote out of years of experience living a life of practical, down-to-earth Christianity. This book is about the transformational journey that all of us must go on if we are to become a rock in God's kingdom. It is written by a true veteran. Candi has been rock solid since the first day I met her, yet constantly growing, walking out her journey with God. She knows what she is writing about!

—APOSTLE BARBARA YODER
FOUNDING APOSTLE AND SENIOR PASTOR
SHEKINAH CHRISTIAN CHURCH
ANN ARBOR, MICHIGAN

Wondering how to make it from a pebble to a rock? Let Dr. Candi MacAlpine take you by the hand and walk you through the life of the apostle Peter. Peter is one of the greatest examples of personal transformation in the Bible, and Candi does a great job of helping you share with Peter the crucial experiences of his life. As you read this book and take time to pray through the questions at the end of each chapter, God will begin to show you how to take the next step in your spiritual journey!

—Dr. Robert Heidler
Apostolic Teacher with Glory of Zion
International Ministries

Peter the Pebble...

PETER THE
ROCK

Peter the Pebble...

PETER THE

ROCK

the journey of
our destiny

CANDI MACALPINE

CREATION
HOUSE

PETER THE PEBBLE...PETER THE ROCK:
THE JOURNEY OF OUR DESTINY
by Dr. Candi MacAlpine
Published by Creation House
A Charisma Media Company
600 Rinehart Road
Lake Mary, Florida 32746
www.charismamedia.com

Unless otherwise noted, all Scripture quotations are from the Holy Bible, New Living Translation, copyright 1996. Used by permission of Tyndale House Publishers, Inc., Wheaton, Illinois 60189. All rights reserved.

Scripture quotations marked NIV are from the Holy Bible, New International Version of the Bible. Copyright © 1973, 1978, 1984, International Bible Society. Used by permission.

Scripture quotations marked NLT are from the Holy Bible, New Living Translation, copyright © 1996, 2004 by Tyndale House Foundation. Used by permission of Tyndale House Publishers Inc., Carol Stream, Illinois, 60188. All rights reserved.

Design Director: Bill Johnson
Cover design by Terry Clifton

Visit the author's website: www.destinytraining.org.

Library of Congress Cataloging-in-Publication Data:
2012937901
International Standard Book Number: 978-1-62136-051-3
E-book International Standard Book Number:
978-1-62136-052-0

While the author has made every effort to provide accurate telephone numbers and Internet addresses at the time of publication, neither the publisher nor the author assumes any responsibility for errors or for changes that occur after publication.

First edition

12 13 14 15 16 — 9 8 7 6 5 4 3 2 1
Printed in Canada

DEDICATION

This book is dedicated to my daughters, Stacy Coleen Daly and Kristina Jayne Lafferty, two of the most incredible women I know—and to think they came from their father and myself is beyond my wildest dream. You have been the most single important tools Jehovah has used to press me forward into my destiny. I love you more than there are words to express it. I honor you both as incredible women of God pressing onward in your own destinies, both uniquely different, both uniquely incredible gifts to the body of Christ. And to put the icing on the cake, you have given us five beautiful grandchildren who are even now because of you pursuing their destiny in their generation. Thank you for the privilege of such beautiful relationships with you both and your families.

TABLE OF CONTENTS

FOREWORD

By Dr. Bill Hamon

CANDI MACALPINE HAS produced a book that is near to the heart of Father God. God created man in His Own image and likeness. It was His desire for Adam and Eve to fill the earth with a race of humanity in God's image and likeness. Adam failed but Jesus came and produced the Church Race. The highest calling of God for mankind is for man to be conformed to the image of Jesus Christ (Romans 8:29).

This book will help you please Your heavenly Father by revealing how you can be transformed to be like Jesus. Every Christian needs to appropriate the truths in this book. It will make improvements in one's life now and throughout eternity.

Thanks Candi for taking the time to share your life and these vital truths with Christ's first love, His Church, which He purchased with His own blood and then sent the Holy Spirit power and grace for each to be like Jesus.

—DR. BILL HAMON
Bishop of Christian International Apostolic Network (CIAN)
Founder of Christian International Ministries Network (CIMN)
Author of *Day of The Saints* and ten other major books
Founder of Vision Church @ Christian International

INTRODUCTION

*W*HY IS IT valuable for you, the reader, to read yet another "Christian" book? Will the words on the following pages and chapters grab you and cause you to evaluate or reevaluate your walk as a disciple of Jesus Christ? Do you hunger for more? Is there a struggle going on inside of you that requires some sort of action on your part? Do you wonder, why am I struggling with certain circumstances or issues in my life?

I want to encourage you, as you begin turning the pages of this manuscript, to be excited as the reader of this book. But also, in this case, I must rather than encourage you, discourage you, because as you begin to wrap your heart and mind around the book, you will be thrust into revelation about the kingdom and your personal destiny, and of course about Peter. A disclaimer would be the knowledge that we are responsible for the truth, once we have acquired it; and in this case, this truth could turn your life upside down—or, in all truth, turn your life right side up. We are called to the kingdom, to walk as Christ followers, to be disciples of the living God.

This is a book to take you not just to the next level, but also even to a level of maturity like the New Testament believers. It's a book to truly transform you into the image of Jesus Christ. It is a book to cause you to weep and cry out, but also to have an understanding of the trials, the pain, the sorrow, the struggles, and the questions that there are no answers for in this life, except in the Word of God and the lives of those who lived it for real. This life is…life. Be it good, be it bad, it is life; and the Spirit of the living God has breathed that life into us. He has given us promise after promise after promise of His plan, of His purpose, and the knowledge that we are heirs of those great promises. We are heirs of a kingdom that we haven't all the answers for yet. My prayer is that this book will cause you to sit back and think. I admonish you to not rush through each chapter, but to pause and think about what you have read and about your life…putting yourself in Peter's place. Put yourself in any-body else's place whose life has been transformed, and you see things in them that you want to see in your life. Jesus promised that He would never leave us or forsake us, even if we try to run away from Him.

In Noah Webster's dictionary of the English language of 1828, the word *transform* is described as "to change the form of, to change the shape or appearance, to metamorphous as a caterpillar is transformed into a butterfly, to change one's substance into another, to transmute, the outcome is sought to transform lead into gold, the theology to change the natural disposition and temper of man from a state of enmity to God and His law into the image of God or into a disposition and temper conforms to the will of God. Romans 12 'be ye transformed by the renewing of your mind, among the mystics it's to change the contemplative soul into a divine substance by which it is lost or swallowed up in the divine nature.'" Noah Webster was a pretty wise man.

I pray this book is a tool to transform you into that beautiful, colorful, majestic, free, and sought after creature totally in sync with its creator. Noah stated, "From a state of enmity to God and His law into the image of God and into a disposition and temper that is conformed totally to the will of God." This is what happened to the apostle Peter. You might say, "Well…that's the great Apostle." Yes, but no…Peter was just like you and me, no different, but he was transformed from a crawling-on-the-ground caterpillar into that majestic butterfly. I pray that this book will transform you from where you are into a place where you are not. I envision this book, like its title, will transform you from a pebble into a rock. Jesus called Peter "the rock." There is so much more to that incredible statement. The key that unlocks the door is that something had to be changed because he did not begin as a rock, but as a pebble, just like you.

And so, will you journey with me into this new place? Take it a bite at a time? You might have to set the book down and wait before going on to the next chapter, and that's OK. I pray that the Word and the Spirit will help you to grow and stretch you, and that you are willing to go where no man has gone before—excuse the pun, you know what I mean (Ha-ha).

Many have chosen to really believe God's Word and promises. They aren't all well recognized or well known, like Bishop Bill Hamon (my spiritual father), who says we are part of the Saint's Movement, where we all get to play. They are just like you and me. We are transformed people who love Jesus and who want to be more than we are today with not only God's blessings, but also His promises fulfilled in our lives, as we journey through this place. Write me a letter or an email; let me know what has happened in your life.

Abundant Blessings sojourner
Candi MacAlpine

Chapter 1

THE JOURNEY BEGINS

$\mathcal{A}$s I BEGIN this journey with you, interestingly enough, I've been flat on my back for eight days now. A week ago, I was doing what Jesus said in caring for the widows, orphans, and the homeless in our community. On Monday evenings we prepare a meal for the needy and homeless in our community. Several local churches have a passion for this and we work with them to do this each Monday night. A week ago Monday night, I was doing that very thing and I fell down three steps. As a result, I had major blunt trauma to my leg that has kept me bedridden for this week, and the doctor said I will stay this way for at least two more weeks.

Anyway, as we begin this journey together into the kingdom of God, and into the discipleship of being a child of the king, wanting to be like Jesus, we can begin here. I make things very personal in my writing because I want you to connect with me and what I'm walking through, as well as what you are walking through. I pray this journey will cause us both to grow. I certainly feel that this is going to be a stretching time. I don't do well having to be incapacitated. I like being in charge, I like being able to do things, and I keep quite busy in one way or another. So as this journey begins with my leg lifted in the air with an ice pack on and pain medication on my nightstand to take if need be, let's delve into the life of the apostle Peter, before he was Peter the Apostle. Let us look at when he was Peter the pebble. He had to begin somewhere, and so do we...so let's begin at the first place.

In any journey, there are always signposts and there is always a path to be taken. In order to follow that path and the signposts we must be prepared in the beginning. The problem with that is we can only prepare for what we have knowledge of, and the rest is that sometimes daunting walk by faith and not by sight. There may be things we will encounter that come as a surprise, or without preparation, or without any knowledge whatsoever. I personally feel, and of course part of this is my personality, that part of the excitement of this journey is not knowing what is around each and every corner.

I am a very organized person. When I travel, I usually begin about a week beforehand to get out the items I will need, starting with clothing, and then going from there. I have found for myself that I am less apt to forget things if I plan ahead. But as I mentioned before, there can be circumstances not under my control that will dictate the need for this or that which is not included in my "suitcase." And so I must improvise, or go to the local establishment of this or that and purchase the item, which I usually pay three times as much for than I would have at home. And of course there is the case of a total change in weather—I came prepared for hot and sultry and all of a sudden there is rain and a twenty-degree drop in the temperature, so I layer and again have to visit the local this or that store.

In any case, this is just a word picture of the journey of our destiny. We can only prepare to the best of our ability;

then we have to put our "suitcase" in the hands of God Almighty, put one foot in front of the other, and begin the journey down the path that stands before us.

Sometimes we choose our own paths and sometimes others put us on a path, but each and every person ever created has and had a path to follow. In the life of Peter we have a beautiful view of his path. The example for us, is that we encounter life's turn of events that will cause us to turn left or right or go straight ahead, and even sometimes back up a bit. When we have taken the wrong path we can turn around and go back to the intersection where we blew it, reevaluate where we turned wrong and then make the adjustment needed, and turn and go down the correct new direction.

Each of us was created for a path, a journey, a destiny. Each is different and handpicked by the mighty "hand" of God, and His promise is that He will take us from beginning destiny to its fulfillment and all the places in between.

Peter's life is the best example of the path from obscurity and lack of vision to being one of the mightiest servants of God of all time in recorded history. In the process he blows it more than the average bear—just like me, incidentally—but in the end, *wow*. I pray we will all find in these pages encouragement, tears, laughter, revelation, hope, balance, truth, and desire to stay on the path to the end and bring others along with us in the process.

The journey to the end of this book may take a while, and that is quite all right. You may need to set it down for a while and ponder and process all that you have read, and then ponder the questions at the end of each chapter. I am a teacher at heart and want my readers to get all they can get out of my writing.

I will ask you the question here at the start. Sit down and spend a considerable time in solitude. Ask the Lord to reveal to you where you are in the process, for you see, we are all about process; our life is a series of processes that take us from one season to another and from one level to another.

I have a philosophy about the religious word, *maturity*. Our goal is certainly maturity, but maturity in what, for what? Is it a job description or an award for accomplishing something? As I look at the Word, especially in Ephesians, it says:

> Then we will no longer be like children, for-ever changing our minds about what we believe because someone has told us something dif-ferent or because someone has cleverly lied to us and made the lie sound like the truth. Instead, we will hold to the truth in love, becoming more and more in every way like Christ, who is the head of his body, the church. Under his direction, the whole body is fitted together per-fectly. As each part does its own special work, it helps the other parts grow, so that the whole body is healthy and growing and full of love [living as Children of Light].
>
> —EPHESIANS 4:14–16

God's plan is for those who have been called as gifts to the church to be a main tool to help us "mature" in our faith, walk, and so forth. He wants us to be kingdom people, not just people who attend a local church and group to be spoon-fed each week. We are to be equipped for the ministry.

OK, let's go back to the previous paragraph about the goal of maturity. It is to bring us up face-to-face with the God of the universe and to have His heart for people and the world. It is to have a vision and purpose that has been spiritually emailed to each individual so that they know why they were created, and why they are walking around on this planet. Each and every one has been prepared, created, thought up, and released to become—as the title of this book infers—not a pebble, but a rock that can fulfill their destiny and change this earth.

There is an incredibly awesome plan that no human could ever conceive of, from the heart and mind of the Creator of the entire universe. He has chosen to partner with that which He has created and given His plan. He has promised to equip us to be successful and leave an imprint on our sphere of influence, just like Peter did.

So let's get on with this journey, and see where we are in the process. Let's move forward, one foot after the other, being really honest. And I do not imply that we take three steps forward and one step back, or whatever formula you have heard, but we move forward. There is no looking back, because yesterday is gone, tomorrow is not ours; we have only today, so let's make the most of it, OK?

Some years ago, the Lord instructed me to not look back. He said, "If you look back at yesterday, or glory in what you did or what took place then, you have the potential of missing what I am taking you into today. You may miss a turn in the road and have to go around the mountain again." I certainly have been around that monolith of a mountain more times than I care to admit, and over more than one issue. I pray you will learn from my blunders and not make the same mistakes. Oh, I realize you will have to make your own blunders that are different from mine. In this process I will probably share some of mine, so you will be able to sidestep them when they loom up in your face. They usually do, you know!

But just before we travel forward into what may look like a time machine, let us look at the days when Jesus walked on this earth, and His encounters and interactions with so many different types of people. Let's check in again and ask. Are you hungering for more? Is there a deep, unsatisfied question or struggle going on inside of you that requires some type of action on your part? Are you struggling with certain circumstances or issues in your life and wondering, "Is this God or the devil?" I believe this book can help you come to some conclusions and answer some questions that have plagued you possibly for years.

Chapter 2

WORKING FOR DAD IN
THE FAMILY BUSINESS

*A*s I STUDY the Word of God, I place myself in the setting of the scenario of the story being told. I look for the
simple message of the passage, but I also look for what has
not been written, what was going on with the people selected
to be a part of this incredible manual for living this life on
this planet. I look for, as they say, what is "between the lines."
I am certainly not adding to the Word of God, but submit-
ting what possibly could have been going on in the lives of
the people besides the information given. I am listening for
Holy Spirit to reveal a deeper understanding than I have had
in the past.

An example, for instance, is Peter. As he lived his daily
life, having not yet met the Messiah Jesus Christ, might he
have said, "I have been working for Dad with my brother in
the family fishing business since I was a kid. That is what
every son does here in Israel. I am an adult now and I have
continued to follow in my father's footsteps, and of course
outdo my brother in the amount of fish I can catch. It can be
a lot of fun at times, but it is also a backbreaking business. It
has to be done so a lot of people can have food for the day"?

This was certainly the cultural custom. These sons were

taught at a very early age all they needed to know to prepare them to be fishermen like their father. I am sure the weather-worn hands of their father spoke volumes, as well as his wind-scarred face, the result of spending years on the open water, even when the waves were close to overtaking them; they may have even lost a boat at some point because a terrible storm arose without warning.

Every day they went out to repeat the same pattern. They would first look at their nets for any tear that would certainly affect their catch of the day. One small hole would make a swift exit for the fish caught in the net, and would certainly make the hole bigger. Also, they couldn't just go down to the local Wal-Mart or Lowe's or Fish and Tackle shop to pick up a new net. They may have made the nets themselves and certainly didn't have money to just cast aside the ones they already were using.

Each day was preparation for the next week or month so that the livelihood they had would follow on for generations, with their table filled with food and some form of fuel in their fireplace to keep them warm on those stormy nights. And in the midst of this family were distinct personalities.

From this "storyline," let's look at what's going on before Peter and Jesus meet face-to-face.

It is important that we read and believe every word in the Bible as absolute truth. The Lord had put to pen, by the power of the Holy Spirit and through His appointed men, His plan and purpose for that which He had created for His glory. We must stay attached to this Word all the days of our lives. I have been studying it for forty years and have only scratched the surface. There is a depth of life and revelation that comes only by the Spirit of God and by our discipline of being in the Word. This is not just reading for the sake of reading, or by a religious ritual because we are supposed to; but to read for life impartations and revelation of God's divine plan for mankind and to give us hope for what we are living in our lives.

It really is no different than the times of the Bible. The cultures are different in many ways, but the truth never changes, God never changes, and His Word never changes. We can live every day of our lives by the truths presented to us. Only by the power of the Spirit can we receive that revelation, and that first comes by faith, which the Word tells us comes by hearing and hearing by the Word of God. I think that is a simple truth anyone can understand. The Holy Spirit will show us if we will only taste and see that the Lord is good, and He wants us to be successful. Remember He is the God of success, and the prophet Jeremiah tells us that His plans for us are for success and not for failure.

Even though we fail at times, I believe that failure is the seedbed of success. Through any failure, He promises to work all things together for good for those He has called to His purposes, and that includes you. If you have believed in the Lord Jesus Christ then you are promised that all things in your life *will* work together for good because you have believed, and will allow, and are called according to His purpose.

Peter is the perfect example of that very thing. He did not begin his life as Peter the Rock. He didn't begin as a rock, and at many times we questioned if he was even a pebble, but Jesus knew because the Father had told him and showed him by prophetic revelation Peter's destiny.

As we look at that very thing, we see ourselves, and we

see the process that all humans must go through to attain the fullness of God's destiny for their lives.

Now do not get me wrong, I certainly am not suggesting any kind of works theology, because we are saved not by works, but by grace and faith. No amount of good works will open the doors of heaven to any person. It never has and it never will.

I hope I have made it clear the journey we are on is to look at the life of one man, Simon. We will then consider the process by which Simon became Peter the Rock, upon which Jesus would build His church. The first time He met Simon, Jesus said, "You are now Simon, but you are Peter inside, and walking with Me will open that door to the fulfillment of your destiny" (author's paraphrase). It wasn't Peter the person whom the church would be built upon, but the spirit of Peter, representing all who would follow after him and walk through the process of transformation and life to become the destiny God intended for each person. Each and every person who has believed in Jesus makes up that organism He has built upon; and we together, corporately, have become that one man to fulfill the Great Commission, as individuals and as a corporate body.

I am not talking about a building, but people who become the church of Jesus Christ in everything they think and do in their life, from the moment they wake in the morning till they lay their head on the pillow at night. Even in the night hours the Spirit will bring dreams and revelation to prepare us for the days to come, and bring the revelation we need in our waking hours.

We are a force to be reckoned with if we will, like Peter, allow the transformation to take place and not be defeated by the rocks in the road we stumble on, or the people who try to defeat us with their words. His Word will come to pass, and His promises will become reality if we will only believe.

Now you may ask, just how much faith must I have to believe? Well the Word is clear: If we only have faith the size of a mustard seed, we can say to any mountain, "Outta here, and melt in the ocean." Now that is a pretty powerful picture, but beyond that it is truth and a promise, so let's get to moving some mountains in our lives and get on with this plan and our destiny.

Just what had taken place before Jesus and Peter (Simon then) met face-to-face? To know that we must go to the Word of God, specifically the Gospels; from each one we get corresponding accounts as well as historical verification of the time and history, and the process that Jesus Himself went through to fulfill His destiny on Planet Earth.

I especially like Luke's translation, which gives a lot more information than the other Gospel accounts. I believe his profession as a doctor and his personality gave us more information to know.

Let's all connect with Peter and his process to our process. We are going to look at all the Gospels and piece together truths that we can appropriate for ourselves and our journey into destiny.

We see the progression, one right after the other: the beginning of the angelic visitations to Zechariah the priest about the birth of his son, John, and then Gabriel's visit to Mary telling her she is favored by the God of the universe. He tells her God is highly pleased with her life, and that she has been selected to be the one who would bring into

the world the Messiah, the Savior, the Redeemer of all mankind. Some assignment for sure!

> When Jesus heard that John had been put
> in prison, he returned to Galilee. Leaving
> Nazareth, he went and lived in Capernaum,
> which was by the lake in the area of Zebulun
> and Naphtali—to fulfill what was said through
> the prophet Isaiah: "Land of Zebulun and land
> of Naphtali, the way to the sea, along the Jordan,
> Galilee of the Gentiles—the people living in
> darkness have seen a great light; on those living
> in the land of the shadow of death a light has
> dawned." From that time on Jesus began to
> preach, "Repent, for the kingdom of heaven is
> near." As Jesus was walking beside the Sea of
> Galilee, he saw two brothers, Simon called Peter
> and his brother Andrew. They were casting
> a net into the lake, for they were fishermen.
> "Come, follow me," Jesus said, "and I will make
> you fishers of men." At once they left their nets
> and followed him.
>
> —MATTHEW 4:12–20, NIV

> Later on, after John was arrested by Herod
> Antipas, Jesus went to Galilee to preach God's
> Good News. "At last the time has come!" he
> announced. "The Kingdom of God is near!
> Turn from your sins and believe this Good
> News!" One day as Jesus was walking along the
> shores of the Sea of Galilee, he saw Simon and
> his brother, Andrew, fishing with a net, for they
> were commercial fishermen. Jesus called out to
> them, "Come, be my disciples, and I will show

you how to fish for people!" And they left their nets at once and went with him.

—MARK 1:14–18

It was now the fifteenth year of the reign of Tiberius, the Roman emperor. Pilate was governor over Judea; Herod Antipas was ruler over Galilee; his brother Philip was ruler over Iturea and Traconitis; Lysanias was ruler over Abilene. Annas and Caiaphas were the high priests. At this time a message from God came to John son of Zechariah, who was living out in the wilderness. Then John went from place to place on both sides of the Jordan River, preaching that people should be baptized to show that they had turned from their sins and turned to God to be forgiven.

—LUKE 3:1–3

Everyone was expecting the Messiah to come soon, and they were eager to know whether John might be the Messiah.

—LUKE 3:15, EMPHASIS ADDED

Then Jesus returned to Galilee, filled with the Holy Spirit's power. *Soon he became well known throughout the surrounding country. He taught in their synagogues and was praised by everyone.*

—LUKE 4:14–15, EMPHASIS ADDED

The beauty of the Scriptures is that we see the historical truth of the geographical areas where Jesus was born and the locations of John the Baptist's birth and ministry. We see who the governing authorities were in each region. These people were all recorded in historical works of ancient history, verifying that Jesus was in those regions where these individuals were government officials.

We also see Jesus moving to Capernaum, fulfilling the prophecy spoken in the Old Testament by the prophet Isaiah. It says the life of Jesus *from the very beginning* was powerful and *all* the people knew about Him, so He was not a stranger to Simon (Peter), his brother, and others there in the fishing business by the sea in Galilee. Also, *everyone* was looking for the Messiah, and everyone means *everyone*, so people were on the lookout for the coming Messiah in their midst. The words I have italicized confirm what I just said. When you lay out from each Gospel certain passages that are not exactly the same in each Gospel, you get a fuller picture; and that, I believe, helps us in our understanding of all that Jesus did and was while on this earth.

We know this family was Hebrew, as is clarified in the Greek translation. So I would imagine at times as they were fishing, but especially as they were mending their nets at the end of the day, they would talk together about this Messiah who would one day show up in their midst and change everything. He would rule over them and the government as they knew it at that time. They heard about it in the synagogue over and over again, so it was not something foreign to any of them.

> When he came to the village of Nazareth, his boyhood home, he went as usual to the synagogue on the Sabbath and stood up to read the Scriptures. The scroll containing the messages of Isaiah the prophet was handed to him, and he unrolled the scroll to the place where it says: "The Spirit of the Lord is upon me, for he

has appointed me to preach Good News to the poor. He has sent me to proclaim that captives will be released, that the blind will see, that the downtrodden will be freed from their oppressors, and that the time of the Lord's favor has come." He rolled up the scroll, handed it back to the attendant, and sat down. Everyone in the synagogue stared at him intently. Then he said, "This Scripture has come true today before your very eyes!"

—LUKE 4:16–21

One day as Jesus was preaching on the shore of the Sea of Galilee, great crowds pressed in on him to listen to the word of God. He noticed two empty boats at the water's edge, for the fishermen had left them and were washing their nets. Stepping into one of the boats, Jesus asked Simon, its owner, to push it out into the water. So he sat in the boat and taught the crowds from there. When he had finished speaking, he said to Simon, "Now go out where it is deeper and let down your nets, and you will catch many fish." "Master," Simon replied, "we worked hard all last night and didn't catch a thing. But if you say so, we'll try again." And this time their nets were so full they began to tear! A shout for help brought their partners in the other boat, and soon both boats were filled with fish and on the verge of sinking. When Simon Peter realized what had happened, he fell to his knees before Jesus and said, "Oh, Lord, please leave me—I'm too much of a sinner to be around you." For he was awestruck by the size of their catch, as were the others with him. His partners, James and John, the sons of Zebedee, were also amazed. Jesus replied to Simon, "Don't be afraid! From now on you'll be fishing for people!" And as soon as they landed, they left everything and followed Jesus.

—Luke 5:1–11

This was the testimony of John when the Jewish leaders sent priests and Temple assistants from Jerusalem to ask John whether he claimed to be the Messiah. He flatly denied it. "I am not the Messiah," he said. "Well then, who are you?" they asked. "Are you Elijah?" "No," he replied. "Are you the Prophet?" "No." "Then who are you? Tell us, so we can give an answer to those who sent us. What do you have to say about yourself?" John replied in the words of Isaiah: "I am a voice shouting in the wilderness, 'Prepare a straight pathway for the Lord's coming!'"

—John 1:19–23

Andrew, Simon Peter's brother, was one of these men who had heard what John said and then followed Jesus. The first thing Andrew did was to find his brother, Simon, and tell him, "We have found the Messiah" (which means the Christ). *Then Andrew brought Simon to meet Jesus. Looking intently at Simon, Jesus said, "You are Simon, the son of John—but you will be called Cephas"* (which means Peter).

—John 1:40–42, emphasis added

Now I am going to attempt to put a puzzle together here for you so that we can see more clearly history, spirituality, life, and life in relationship with Jesus, and how He orchestrates our destiny.

I have given you all the passages so they are easy for you to reference as we lay them upon one another to get a better picture of Peter's beginnings as a follower of Christ and soon-to-be apostle, and the first to engage in "insert foot in mouth disease," as we call it in slang terms. He lacked the maturity or experience to know, see, and believe.

Let's back up a minute and look at Jesus's past. He was born and raised in the home of Joseph and Mary, which included brothers and sisters and a normal childhood. On their way to Passover, Jesus leaves the extended family and friends traveling to go to the synagogue, and is found there teaching, the elders wondering how He is so wise and knowledgeable of the Scriptures.

We see Him next going out into the wilderness, where He is tempted by the devil for forty days. Jesus comes out hungry, but puts His strength in the living Word and is victorious. He then connects with His cousin, John the Baptist, who begins to prophesy the moment he sees Him, declaring, "This is the Messiah, and I am not worthy to even untie His sandals." Realize that to untie a guest's shoes was a chore left to slaves in households. Remember also, there were no asphalt roads. Everywhere was dirt, so the feet of people coming into the homes was filthy to say the least, notwithstanding any cuts, disease, and so forth on individuals' feet.

The servant would have to first untie the sandals before washing the feet of the individual. This was a backbreaking, filthy job. John was humbling himself, realizing the people would understand his statement due to their culture, and hopefully this would cause them to see and believe that this Jesus was truly the Messiah they had all been waiting for.

From here Jesus asks John to baptize Him, and with reluctance, John does so. From here we step into our purpose, connecting Jesus and Peter.

How can we apply this in our lives?

When I look at the personality of Jesus and the character of the Father, I know He always has plenty of different ways of making connections with us. His heart of love will stop at nothing to make that first connection and to reach out with a desire for relationship. It is then up to us to respond and make the connection, and then begin to build the relationship. I am sure you have heard the statement, "God has given us a free will and He will not invade that." Well, yes, we do have a free will; but God in His wisdom is able to orchestrate circumstances and situations that make a way for us to say yes to His desires and destiny for our lives.

I know in my own life He has used every conceivable way to get my attention, in ways that showed me without any question how much He loved me, or how important it was for me to make decisions that would impact my destiny. Peter was the same, and God had already made provision through many circumstances, even just the knowing about Jesus in the region and of the miracles. You know word gets around quick when signs and wonders, miracles, and people coming back from the dead happen. It doesn't take a newspaper or even the Internet in these days for the word to get out. I choose to believe that Peter was already pondering about this Jesus and what He was doing.

We know about Peter's "hoof-in-mouth disease" (and many, myself included, also are afflicted with this disease), and how much trouble he could get in with his quick responses to circumstances. His first encounter with Jesus was no different. Here they all are, on the seashore, and this miracle Man shows up and begins to talk to Peter and his bros and dad. In Peter's quick mind he must have thought, "Why not? It's something new, and fishing is really hard work—long hours, severe cold and extreme heat, and no promise of any catch every day."

But in the heart of the Father was Peter's destiny. Don't you think He knew of Peter's quick responses, sometimes really bad? But that was not an issue, just like with us. He knows everything about us; just as a reminder, He created us, He knows the destiny He has planned for us, and He gives hundreds of opportunities for us to step into our destiny, like stepping into a new suit and living on the cutting edge of what we now know is the kingdom of God and the purpose of all eternity.

So we end this chapter with a major shift for Peter in his destiny. He and his family thought they would spend the rest of their lives just fishing like they had done every day up to this day, but God....

Be ready. If you haven't encountered the Lord in a major way, I would say this may be your day!

TIME TO PAUSE

1. What happens today could change your whole perspective; look for it.

2. Why not today? Just like He did with Peter, He invades our life when we least expect it.

3. What can you do to prepare ahead of time? Be practical.

4. You might even journal what your responses might be.

Chapter 3

WHO IS THIS MAN TELLING ME TO COME BE A FISHER OF MEN?

As Jesus was walking beside the Sea of Galilee, he saw two brothers, Simon called Peter and his brother Andrew. They were casting a net into the lake, for they were fishermen. "Come, follow me," Jesus said, "and I will make you fishers of men." At once they left their nets and followed him. Going on from there, he saw two other brothers, James son of Zebedee and his brother John. They were in a boat with their father Zebedee, preparing their nets. Jesus called them, and immediately they left the boat and their father and followed him. Jesus went throughout Galilee, teaching in their synagogues, preaching the good news of the kingdom, and healing every disease and sickness among the people. News about him spread all over Syria, and people brought to him all who were ill with various diseases, those suffering severe pain, the demon-possessed, those having seizures, and the paralyzed, and he healed them. Large crowds from Galilee, the Decapolis, Jerusalem, Judea and the region across the Jordan followed him.

[MATTHEW 4:18–5:1, NIV]

*D*ID JESUS KNOW who these brothers were as He walked along the seashore of Galilee? Well, since we know that He did nothing lest He saw the Father doing, it I would say yes. I am sure Jesus and the Father had conversations about those first disciples, and Jesus was prepared to engage them as He came across them in His journey to Jerusalem. He knew where they were when He met them, and He knew the destiny the Father had planned for them in the days and years ahead, even beyond the Cross.

I am sure there was something about this man Jesus that Simon Peter sensed, and was drawn to Him on many levels. Peter was a man's man, so I do not believe that he would have been drawn to less than a manly man, even rugged to some degree. He knew who He was because of the talk all around the region. He knew of the healings and also the gossip of who was this man, His teachings, and the miracles that followed Him on a daily basis. I don't think he was just tired of the family business, but down deep in the deepest part of Peter was a small stone of destiny. He may not have ever even considered it possible, but there may have always been a nagging thought, or maybe day-dream of a different life, one that did not consist of getting up early in the morning to go out in the cold or heat of whatever season it was, to throw the family nets over the side of the boat, and with calloused hands pull them back in, hopefully with a load of fish to sell that day in the town marketplace. Did Jesus in His statement to Peter touch that secret hidden possibility of more fulfillments? I choose to believe He did. And I choose to believe it is no different for you and me when we encounter this Jesus Man for the first time with eyes filled with destiny yet to be realized in us.

We all must begin somewhere, and it is usually at the beginning. This was Peter's beginning of a new chapter of his destiny—and what a destiny it would be. I want to stop and encourage you right here that you are somewhere in the process of your own destiny, formed by the Father before the foundations of the earth. He is watching as it unfolds before you and before Him.

I could write so many testimonies. It would take up an entire volume—and that would be only my personal encounters. And of course we have an entire Book called the Bible that journals the destiny of men and women throughout history, and so many more that are written and unwritten. I want you to focus on you and where you are in this process. What is your next chapter? You wouldn't be reading this book if you did not have some interest in the subject matter.

You have realized you have a dream, and that dream has been planted in you by God. He promises to participate with you in this dream and provide you with everything you will ever need to fulfill it. It will not be a yellow brick road like in *The Wizard of Oz*, and it will not always look like a piece of the dream, but it is nonetheless. I choose to believe that my heavenly Father is not a man that He would lie, and that His promises are yes and amen. He will follow me like a hound dog down every path I walk and give me direction as I ask, and even when I do not ask. He promises to make the crooked places straight, and He promises to be a lamp to our feet and a light to our path. We have no excuse but to move forward.

That dream that you are carrying can be anything. It includes a wish book of the greatest magnitude and the whole world in which to accomplish it, all backed by the kingdom of God. It may be a judgeship, or to become an incredible actor or actress. It might even be caring for small children on a daily basis. It is not limited to the sphere of the organized church and its purpose but includes all that Jehovah has created for His pleasure. Remember it is His design and as long as we have established it as a kingdom place and He has confirmed its existence, then stand back and watch destiny explode exponentially.

Jesus will always talk to us in ways that we can relate to. He did this with Peter when He said, "I will make you fishers of men" (Matt. 4:19). They could totally understand what this meant and it was certainly intriguing to them.

> When Jesus heard that John had been arrested, he left Judea and returned to Galilee. But instead of going to Nazareth, he went to Capernaum, beside the Sea of Galilee, in the region of Zebulun and Naphtali. This fulfilled Isaiah's prophecy: "In the land of Zebulun and of Naphtali, beside the sea, beyond the Jordan River—in Galilee where so many Gentiles live— the people who sat in darkness have seen a great light.
>
> And for those who lived in the land where death casts its shadow, a light has shined." From then on, Jesus began to preach, "Turn from your sins and turn to God, because the Kingdom of Heaven is near." One day as Jesus was walking along the shore beside the Sea of Galilee, he saw two brothers—Simon, also called Peter, and Andrew—fishing with a net, for they were commercial fishermen. Jesus called out to them, "Come, be my disciples, and I will show you how to fish for people!" And they left their nets at once and went with him.
>
> —Matthew 4:12–20

I want to add here the historical events that were happening right before Jesus and Peter came face to face. We clearly see through the Scriptures that a prophecy was also being fulfilled. Jesus was walking in His destiny and fulfilling the prophetic word of the prophet Isaiah. It is said that many who were in darkness, beginning in the land of Zebulun down to the sea in Galilee, have now seen a great light. Peter was one of those who sat in darkness, and the moment the Light appeared on the scene he saw that light and followed it into his destiny and purpose for which he was created.

Peter had no idea what the days ahead would bring to him and the daily face-to-face discipleship he would have with the Jesus Man, and his "hoof-in-mouth disease." He also had no idea of the agony He would suffer by his own hand, or the depth of forgiveness possible from that same Man.

From that place came a giant of a man preaching with conviction, power, authority, and humility because of all he had walked through in the time he walked with Jesus and beyond.

Peter's first encounter with his destiny takes place right where he lives, right where he is comfortable with his life. Isn't that just like Jesus, to just show up in our lives right in our own comfortable digs? With a good job, funds coming in to live for a few weeks or month, lifetime friends and family to hang out with? Life is good, and then like a comet out of the sky, *everything* changes.

TIME TO PAUSE

1. Take time here to think back to your first encounter with Jesus. Remind yourself of all that happened there, your emotions, your questions, and your thoughts as your life took a sharp detour into your destiny.

2. Journal some questions you might have had or thought at the time. Do you have some of the answers? What are they?

3. Begin a journal chronicling your destiny with God beginning wherever you feel it needs to begin.

4. Just spend some time in your secret place with Him. Let Him talk to you about you today and where you have come to now.

5. Ask for a fresh encounter with your Destiny Weaver.

Chapter 4

JUST MINDING MY OWN BUSINESS

One day as Jesus was preaching on the shore of the Sea of Galilee, great crowds pressed in on him to listen to the word of God. He noticed two empty boats at the water's edge, for the fishermen had left them and were washing their nets. Stepping into one of the boats, Jesus asked Simon, its owner, to push it out into the water. So he sat in the boat and taught the crowds from there. When he had finished speaking, he said to Simon, "Now go out where it is deeper and let down your nets, and you will catch many fish." "Master," Simon replied, "we worked hard all last night and didn't catch a thing. But if you say so, we'll try again." And this time their nets were so full they began to tear! A shout for help brought their partners in the other boat, and soon both boats were filled with fish and on the verge of sinking. When Simon Peter realized what had happened, he fell to his knees before Jesus and said, "Oh, Lord, please leave me—I'm too much of a sinner to be around you." For he was awestruck by the size of their catch, as were the others with him. His partners, James and John, the sons of Zebedee, were also amazed. Jesus replied to Simon, "Don't be afraid! From now on you'll be fishing for people!" And as soon as they landed, they left everything and followed Jesus.

[LUKE 5:1–11]

*W*HAT I LOVE about the Gospels is that each one gives a perspective on the same scenario. I am sure Holy Spirit purposely did that to cause us to see that different vessels communicate encounters and circumstances a little differently. When you put them all together you get a fuller picture of what the Father is communicating through the Word.

Jesus was preaching close to where the guys were working on their nets. They had come in from a day of fishing. The typical procedure done each and every time they returned from the sea was to clean and repair their nets for the following day. If they did not take care of these vital implements of their trade, they would lose the potential of a great catch and not make any money for that day, plus tarnish their reputation a bit for not being on top of their business production.

People were following Jesus, holding on to every word. According to plan, Jesus walks right along the water's edge and sees the boys working, and just steps into one of their boats. We need to interject again from the Gospels what isn't reported in the others. This is not Simon Peter's first encounter with Jesus the Christ.

> Andrew, Simon Peter's brother, was one of these men who had heard what John said and then followed Jesus. The first thing Andrew did was to find his brother, Simon, and tell him, "We have found the Messiah" (which means the Christ). Then Andrew brought Simon to meet Jesus. Looking intently at Simon, Jesus said, "You are Simon, the son of John—but you will be called Cephas" (which means Peter).
> —JOHN 1:40–42

Jesus already knows this is Peter, having been introduced to him through his brother, Andrew, who had been impacted and realized this was and is the Christ they have been waiting for. He asks him to push off the shore. Now I look at all things from a spiritual perspective, and this is no different. Jesus knew exactly what He was doing and what was coming next. I am sure Peter was dumbfounded and didn't quite know what to say to Jesus as He was stepping into his boat and telling him to take it out into the water. He had heard the words Jesus spoke over him, prophesying to him his name and who his father was. He also prophesied that his name would be changing to Peter the rock. Peter just may not have been able to do any differently than obey. He saw the crowds; he saw the "Light" that had just planted His sandaled feet into his boat, and moved into that next spiritual encounter of his destiny.

Understand also that Peter, his brother, and family were regular attendees at the local synagogue. They had heard the prophecies of the coming Messiah and the characteristics that defined Him. Things were beginning to snowball out of man's control. And we do so like to control things.

Now Peter is in the boat with Jesus as Jesus is teaching the multitude that has been following Him for days. I am sure Peter was speechless and for maybe the first time he had really heard Jesus and was magnetically drawn to what He was telling them.

Remember fishing boats of this time were not huge, so he was probably within touching distance from Jesus as He taught the people, possibly using a metaphor of fishing and the kingdom of God.

The Sea of Galilee (along with the entire Mediterranean Sea) was a major source of food, fish specifically. It was a major part of their diet. Jesus used this analogy about fish and fishing numerous times in teaching those gathered about the kingdom, their personal destiny in Him, and His purpose for coming. Just think how many of Jesus's disciples were fishermen; possibly seven: Peter, Andrew, Philip, James, John, Thomas, Nathanael. Think of the different parables and messages Jesus gave using fish and fishermen as word pictures the people could relate to.

Back to Jesus and Peter in the boat. Jesus has finished His message to the crowd. He turns to Peter, who I bet was about to take the boat back to the shore. He had completed the task the Master had asked of him. He was also tired from an entire night of fishing with not much to show for it. His dad and family are not happy; no fish, no money, no house payment!

Isn't it just like Jesus when we are at our worst, feeling crummy about some situation, and He shows up on the scene and completely changes the subject.

Peter was feeling pretty good about his service to the Man he had heard so much about, but just as he is about to put the oar in the water, Jesus interjects: "Hey Peter, go out where it is deeper; put your nets down and let's do some fishing together." I am sure Peter is astounded by this request. He knows Jesus is not part of the local fisherman's local 777, but again honoring who He is, he obliges Him. What he doesn't know is that Jesus is teaching him first-hand how they together will expand the kingdom of God fishing for men. Destiny has taken a huge step forward and Peter doesn't even know it yet.

With respect, Peter responds, even calling Him "Master." Sometimes our heart responds without even asking our permission, and we sovereignly step into a God moment and speak before we realize what has happened. He responds, "We have been out all night and didn't catch a single fish." But being a respectful man, he goes ahead, with just a hint of faith combined with the request of the Master, and puts the nets back in the water. Lo and behold they can't even pull the nets in because they are so full of fish, so full and heavy they are tearing the nets. Even though Peter's first response to their partners in the other boat is "Help," something was happening and Peter unknowingly set his sails to walk the waters of life and destiny with the King of kings and Lord of lords.

There were so many fish that both boats were full to the max, almost on the verge of sinking. They haven't even made it to the shore to unload the boats before Peter responds and falls to his knees before Jesus with humility, realizing how sinful a man he is before this anointed Teacher.

This miracle was the first power evangelism activation! And it really produced fruit, because the Scriptures report in the Luke passage that all of them were awestruck by the miracle and wondered about their encounter with this Man they had heard so much about.

Fear grabs a hold of us when we realize we are in the presence of God and His power, which is a normal response for us humans. Peter and the others responded likewise. Jesus immediately tells them to not be afraid and prophesies to them that from this moment forward they would be fishing for men's souls for the rest of their lives.

Fear is the first threat to our destiny and will continue to try and trap you every time you step out into deeper waters of your destiny. Fear will do anything possible to sidestep you, to divert you, to cause you to just give up and not move toward becoming the rock Jesus intends you to be. You must first realize it is the first line of attack of the enemy, and then take the bull by the horns and declare the Word of God that deals completely with any and all fear:

> For God has not given us a spirit of fear and timidity, but of power, love, and self-discipline.
> —2 TIMOTHY 1:7

You can take this scripture to the bank and keep drawing on it every day if necessary because new schemes of fear will assault you along the path of that destiny. You must be wise, ready to ward off its tiny little interjections.

Jesus has made you strong in the power of His might. In ourselves we can do nothing—get over your bad self. It is through the indwelling Holy Spirit that we can do all things through Christ, who strengthens us day in and day out. Peter walked this out throughout his life, conquering every spirit of fear that raised its ugly head.

After this chance encounter with fear, the whole gang—Peter, Andrew, James and John, the sons of Zebedee—left everything that very day and followed Jesus for the rest of their lives.

For many, life simply moves forward day by day, no matter what the circumstances. We live, we work, we move forward. I must ask the question, Where are you in your forward momentum? It was no different for Simon Peter and his brother, but here ancient prophecy invades the simplicity of life and climatic circumstances change everything, and a rippling effect begins to skip across the timeline of the universe and that person's destiny. The principle is the same and continues across the time line of God's design. Be alert to what seems like a chance encounter, but is in reality a bold step of faith into your destiny.

TIME TO PAUSE

1. Begin to chronicle—yes you can, just take some time—the steps the Lord has already begun in you. There is always a process. You just may not have seen what has been the plan of God for your destiny quite as clearly as you can now.

2. Establish a new mind-set to walk in new levels of faith for the next encounters that will form your next season of destiny and purpose.

3. Write a letter to the Lord promising to do this very thing, with some specifics if possible. Give it to someone and have them mail it to you in six months. See what has happened in the ensuing time and chronicle it.

4. Be honest with yourself and Him. What arenas of fear assault you? Begin to deal with them; cast them out and declare your freedom from every fear that tries to stop you from moving forward.

Chapter 5

ON THE ROAD AGAIN
WITH JESUS

Telling Stories and Visiting My Mother-In-Law

When Jesus arrived at Peter's house, Peter's mother-in-law was sick in bed with a high fever. But when Jesus touched her hand, the fever left her. Then she got up and prepared a meal for him.

[MATTHEW 8:14–15, NLT]

*A*s WE BEGIN this truly committed (or so we think) journey with Jesus, we encounter many situations along the path. Sometimes in the beginning we do not even see the setup He has orchestrated for our training in His school of the kingdom.

Peter and the boys see before their own eyes not stories from others in the next town, but firsthand. The healing of a leper astounds them, and then Jesus instructs the healed man to follow the Law of Moses and go to the priest with the required offering. Oh, and by the way, do not say anything on your way there. It was not about Jesus being recognized, but about waking the people to the fact that God heals.

Jesus many times rocked the boat of the priests' and Pharisees' mind-sets and nailed them in the condition of their hearts. But here He wants a greater impact by staying in the line of the law. Sometimes we need to do this so that down the road there will be a greater impact.

Their next encounter is the Centurion soldier with a very sick little boy. Jesus immediately discerns the man's faith. Certainly a Gentile could not have the faith of a Jew?

They then arrive at their destination, Peter's home, where his wife, family, and his mother-in-law are waiting. It was a bummer of a family get-together, as evidently they had planned a big party, but Peter's mother in law—who certainly must have been the chef of the day—was ill in bed with a high fever. Jesus immediately took care of the fever and she instantly got up and fixed, I am sure, an awesome Jewish Kosher meal. Wish I had been there.

We must be ready in season and out of season to be always prepared for the unexpected need that crosses our path. Jehovah has already seen it and has sent us that way in order to be matured, to be available, and to be light, salt, and full of power.

I have learned that as I make my schedule for the day and in my travels, God may shift me to the complete opposite direction. I may have a day planned at the computer doing admin stuff, or plan to deep clean my house. Then the first phone call comes, and I at first fidget because my agenda has been interrupted by my Master. I settle down and step out of the flesh and into the Spirit and minister life, or healing, or a prophetic word, or just listen to a hurting heart. Jesus never turned away from a need; He always used it to train His disciples, even though so many times they just did not get it. We are no different. Jesus and the Father and Holy Spirit never give up on us. Boy am I glad they did not give up on Peter and the boys, and I am so glad they did not give up on me either. I am sure you feel the same. I cannot tell you how many times I have missed it, each time realizing I have, and my heart hurts because more than anything I didn't hear Him or realize I was His instrument for someone else's destiny.

Life is continual and stuff happens. I wonder if Peter was worried about how his wife and family would perceive all this. Well, Jesus took care of all that when He healed his mother-in-law's fever. If she was questioning before, she sure was not after, as is clear when she immediately began the meal.

Let us look at this sometimes scary scenario. Family can really be encouraging and loving about our walk with Jesus, but they can also be the exact opposite. We have to get past that by keeping our eyes on Jesus and His destiny for our lives.

Things were moving quickly, day after day healing strangers, and casting out demons from the local trouble-maker. Your destiny will always take you around corners to run smack dab into someone or something you were not expecting. Walking the path of our destiny is not knowing everything or how to handle every circumstance, but it is being willing to be available and embracing His agenda for the kingdom's sake. It is being willing to lay our wants aside for Him.

In Matthew 8:18–22 Jesus speaks to His disciples what I would call a wake up call, the first of many. We are told to count the cost of following Christ. Do not kid yourself;

there is a cost for sure, and no one knows the magnitude of it until they are faced with the facets of it on our path of life. Remember, He already knew the destiny of the disciples He was walking with. He also knows our destiny, and He is walking with us just like He walked with them. He is willing to speak the truth even when we do not fully understand. He tells them, speaking specifically as one of the teachers of religious law, that He would never have a home or even a place to sleep temporarily. He wasn't saying we cannot have homes, but that there is a price for following Him, so you need to consider it before you say yes.

On the other side are so many promises of His helping us, with the power of Holy Spirit to be with us and help us make it to the top. He even tells one of the disciples to not even go home to bury his father. He is not being insensitive toward this disciple, but speaking the reality that if we are going to follow Him, He must be first—really first—in our lives. He already knew that this man's father and family were spiritually dead.

I think it is so wonderful that after all that has taken place within the last days or weeks, He gets into the boat to cross the sea with the fishermen. A huge storm blows and they are terrified. He immediately deals with the spirit of fear that that has grabbed their hearts and speaks to their little faith. He then takes authority over the storm and again, by example, shows that storms and fear are no giants against the authority of Jehovah. Declarations made by simple faith will stop a storm in its tracks. I have done it a number of times, be it rain, snow, destructive winds, or earthquakes; whatever it is, we have been given the authority to stop destruction that is not in the plan of Jehovah.

Down the road they will experience a commissioning by Jesus and then He will tell them that they have all authority over all things and everything the enemy wants to throw into their face.

TIME TO PAUSE

1. Write down declarations you have made in the past. If you have never made declarations before, start today. He has given you all authority to use His name to stop in its tracks anything that has interrupted the will of the Father.

2. What has hindered you in the past from your path of destiny? Write it down and remember it so you will not allow it to happen again.

Chapter 6

PRESUMPTION IS PETER'S MIDDLE NAME—AND MINE TOO

Matthew 16:22-32, Mark 8:32-33—rebuking Jesus;
Luke 8:45—the woman with the issue of blood;
John 13:6-11—refuses to let Jesus wash his feet.

$\mathcal{P}$ETER WAS THE master of presumption, and he didn't stop after the first confrontation with Jesus on the matter. It was part of his character that had to be encountered again and again until it was flushed out of his life. It is no different for us. The problem is that many times when we come face-to-face with this monster we cut and run. We give up on ourselves and our purpose in life...it usually takes years to form, but what have we got but time?

It is also like the diamond found in the dirt—rough and not very pretty, and certainly no facets to reflect the light inside. Diamonds in the rough never look like the finished exquisite valuable gem so sought after by many. It takes precision and training to be a diamond cutter, precisely setting the tool that will cut each facet at its perfect spot to reflect the incredible light inside waiting to be set free to shine. It takes precision to cut the facets in the beginning, as well as in the middle stages and finally the finished product. It is not until it is a finished work that we see the clarity, the beauty, and the great value that was not seen in its initial form. The diamond is forged through great heat and pressure before it can become the hardest material that it is. A master diamond cutter can see through all the debris, all the clouded parts, and the fractures hidden from the naked eye. His years of training have given him an eye to see and be able to reveal the beauty, clarity, and value of that piece of quartz rock.

I Must Go to Jerusalem

In Matthew and Mark, Jesus tells the disciples again that He must go to Jerusalem, and He will die. Peter slips right up with his love and caring. He doesn't get the message, and rebukes Jesus, telling Him this just will not happen and that He should not talk about it because he (Peter) will not allow it to happen. Jesus immediately addresses the demon spirit attached to Peter, and the arrogance of his worldly perspective, worldly wisdom and knowledge, and nails that mind-set Peter has walked in all his life. Peter was speaking from a human point of view and not the spiritual truth of God's kingdom, and certainly not the Word of God.

Like Peter, we must at times be confronted with this same human malady. It must be broken off of us so that we can see with the eyes of the Spirit and not the flesh. We must grasp that our understanding of the kingdom of God is not life and food and whatever comes our way. We are spiritual beings, created by the only Creator. We were created for a divine and specific purpose, and bought with a price, by which we are to live our lives for Him and Him alone. We must be conformed to His image, and it takes situations like this to bring the transformation. It usually is not comfortable, but if we will accept it we will receive the transformation needed to take us into a new season of serving the kingdom and the King and, like Peter, walk in the fullness of our destiny.

In the Luke passage Peter challenges Jesus's statement asking who touched Him. Jesus knew there was a crowd of people and everyone wanted to touch Him. He wanted the fullness of this encounter to be seen, heard, and received by the multitudes following Him—especially the Jews, because the woman was a Jew. She grabbed His *tallit* and the "wings" where the names of God are represented as tied knots used for prayer. She grabbed the one that is *Jehovah Rophe*, our Healer, and was instantly healed. She knew exactly what she was doing, and nothing was going to stop her from getting healed. She was at the end of her ability to find healing. She turned to her only hope.

We are so precious to Jehovah and He will use all things to bring us up higher and higher into the fulfillment of the character of His Son, the Messiah. We all want to be like Jesus, we just chafe at the process. It is inevitable and we will continue on this path until He comes or we go, whichever comes first.

We are in the school of preparation for eternal ruling and reigning with Him throughout all eternity. Remember what he told us? He said we would rule and reign with Him over the nations. I consider that quite huge in the realm of my earthly understanding, but I also know I do not understand everything. As I walk daily in His presence and continue my pursuit as a student of God's written Word, and as I follow the leading of Holy Spirit, He will work all things together for me and what is good. He will make me into the image that I so passionately desire. We, like Peter, are on the path, narrow as it may be, to a greater glory than we could ever envision or imagine. Our responsibility is to submit to the process, take the corrections, stay in the boot camp of training so that we will be fully ready to encounter all circumstances and situations, and be like all the examples we see in the Book of Hebrews' hall of faith. We really are like them; do not think you cannot attain to that high calling. We can and will accomplish all if we just are willing. Jehovah is just looking for some willing participants to build His kingdom into all that has already been ordained.

I do not know about you, but I want to ride right alongside my Lord and Savior, making the kingdoms of this world into the kingdoms of our God, and serving our Creator with all that we have and even more. You are a vessel of honor, and you have resident within your spirit strength, a power, a knowing that will take you into whatever comes your way. And you will be victorious, because He says we are victorious In Matthew and Mark, Jesus tells the disciples again that He must go to Jerusalem, and He will die. Peter slips right up with his love and caring. He doesn't get the message, and rebukes Jesus, telling Him this just will not happen and that He should not talk about it because he (Peter) will not allow it to happen. Jesus immediately addresses the demon spirit attached to Peter, and the arrogance of his worldly perspective, worldly wisdom and knowledge, and nails that mind-set Peter has walked in all his life. Peter was speaking from a human point of view and not the spiritual truth of God's kingdom, and certainly not the Word of God. Like Peter, we must at times be confronted with this same human malady. It must be broken off of us so that we can see with the eyes of the Spirit and not the flesh. We must grasp that our understanding of the kingdom of God is not life and food and whatever comes our way. We are spiritual beings, created by the only Creator. We were created for a divine and specific purpose, and bought with a price, by which we are to live our lives for Him and Him alone. We must be conformed to His image, and it takes situations like this to bring the transformation. It usually is not comfortable, but if we will accept it we will receive the transformation needed to take us into a new season of serving the kingdom and the King and, like Peter, walk in the fullness of our destiny.

In the Luke passage Peter challenges Jesus's statement asking who touched Him. Jesus knew there was a crowd of people and everyone wanted to touch Him. He wanted the fullness of this encounter to be seen, heard, and received by the multitudes following Him—especially the Jews, because the woman was a Jew. She grabbed His *tallit* and the "wings" where the names of God are represented as tied knots used for prayer. She grabbed the one that is *Jehovah Rophe*, our Healer, and was instantly healed. She knew exactly what she was doing, and nothing was going to stop her from getting healed. She was at the end of her ability to find healing. She turned to her only hope.

We are so precious to Jehovah and He will use all things to bring us up higher and higher into the fulfillment of the character of His Son, the Messiah. We all want to be like Jesus, we just chafe at the process. It is inevitable and we will continue on this path until He comes or we go, whichever comes first.

We are in the school of preparation for eternal ruling and reigning with Him throughout all eternity. Remember what he told us? He said we would rule and reign with Him over the nations. I consider that quite huge in the realm of my earthly understanding, but I also know I do not understand everything. As I walk daily in His presence and continue my pursuit as a student of God's written Word, and as I follow the leading of Holy Spirit, He will work all things together for me and what is good. He will make me into in Him, and through Him we can do all things.

THINK ABOUT IT

1. List your dreams of your very best in serving Him.

2. List what you think may be blocking your accomplishing this.

3. Set some goals for the next six months and keep a record of successes and failures. Remember that failure is the seedbed of success.

Chapter 7

MATURITY TAKING HOLD OF PETER'S LIFE—OR IS IT FOOLISHNESS?

Matthew 14:28–31—Peter walks on water. A real test of faith for Peter as he "steps out of the boat" on his own to get to Jesus.

*N*ow this is the ultimate test of faith—or is it foolishness? Well, depending on your mind-set you choose. But the right answer is the ultimate test of faith. I believe this was a juncture in Peter's life that was setting him up for the days when he became the force of God upon a godless people and preached with such authority and power that thousands were saved. It is the beginning of the place that took Peter to his destiny, and the statements in the Word of God that even his shadow healed people.

I am desirous to have such maturity and faith that even my shadow would bring healing to individuals. Let me challenge you to think of what it took for Peter to first see the situation and then make the decision to step out of the boat. He had to dig down really deep to pull up that magnitude of faith. He knew where they were—in the middle of a lot of cold, deep water—and he knew how many men had died in that same water when swept over the side of their fishing boats and engulfed by the tons of water, taken to the bottom of the sea to become fish food. Do not kid yourself; all that was there in his memory, so it took—excuse the pun—a boatload of faith to step out. What will it take for you to dig down deep and step out of the boat?

This is such a poignant picture encouraging us to do the very same thing in our own lives. The situation will be different. You may realize what faith you have stepped into and panic; then, looking at yourself in the flesh, realize this is impossible, but Jesus grabs your hand, just as He did Peter's, and pulls you up.

Let yourself dream of that day when you are willing to step out of the boat; in fact, why not consider it today or tomorrow? Do not let it get away from you, and do not let the enemy taunt and tell you that you cannot do it or that it is impossible. That is a lie; the Word says that with God all things are possible in Him (Matt. 19:26), and we are in Him, so we can do the impossible. It will produce a fruit beyond your imagination and you will be on the railroad tracks of destiny, secured on those tracks of Holy Spirit directing you forward to your destination. Nothing can derail you, except you yourself. You can take yourself off those tracks and be dead weight in the sands of life. I promise you they will try to bog you down. Keep on those tracks and keep pouring the fuel of the Word, of prayer, of obedience into that engine and let it roar down the tracks.

Keepin' Our Eyes on Jesus or Deep in the Drink We Go!

How many times have we in our heightened spiritual condition taken a step of faith only to drop into the drink? Even though we did not drown, we came up sputtering the water that we sucked in when we tried to breathe under water. It is times like this when we truly do exercise childlike faith, even though we may stumble and fall; but He promises to pick us up. Then we get our eyes back on Jesus and do begin to walk out on water, which we never thought we were capable of doing.

"Hoof-in-Mouth Disease" (Matt. 26:33–35; Luke 22:32–41, John 13:36–38)

Interesting, isn't it, that three of the Gospels tell on Peter again? Funny, in a way. I am sure he was the brunt of many of bouts of laughter due to his "tendency" to speak when he should not have spoken. Oh Peter, Peter…or should I say, Oh, Candi, Candi! How we all are carriers of "hoof-in-mouth disease." And if you think you are not a carrier, well, we can deal with that spirit!

Interesting that James, the brother of Jesus, was very clear about these circumstances and the unruly tongue. It gets us into trouble every time it is not kept under control, and we continue to grapple with this condition that James tells us is incapable of being controlled (James 3:8). Proverbs tells us that too many words produce sin (Prov. 10:19). Wow, I keep that one close at hand and try to implement it as much as possible. So what is the key? Well, to be honest I do not know, other than to think more and speak less. If I do not let the words out of my mouth, maybe eventually I will have greater control and not be so sickly with "hoof-in-mouth disease."

We are really moving forward in this process and are more than halfway through our example of Peter's life and process. You and he are not just pebbles anymore, but you are gathering strength, power, authority, faith, knowledge, and experience, and are moving at a faster speed than before.

MATTHEW 17:1–4
THE TRANSFIGURATION

As we delve into this heaven on earth story, let me go down a rabbit trail in regards to our transformation. We are constantly in a flux of transformation from the moment of conception to the day we leave this earth. Sometimes it is hard to get your mind around this phenomenon because you cannot grab it like a phone. It is like the wind and it will not be contained, for it is the stuff of spiritual DNA. It takes us from that moment of conception when the God of the universe decides it is time for us to come to earth. This is similar to when He said the same words regarding Jesus's time to be conceived in a woman's womb, with the miracle of the Creator of life and the egg of a woman created by that same Creator of life.

It is certainly beyond my mental capacity to understand, but that is true of so many things in my existence, because again I must remind myself I am the created being and He is the incredible, undeniable, and beyond my ability to conceive *God* of all things. I am like a child in many things, looking at them in awe, and the majesty and beauty. When I stand in the forest of the High Sierras where I live, the uncountable hues of green in nature overwhelm me. I have tried and it just doesn't work because there are too many to count; plus when the light of the sun hits them, it changes the hue again.

I am forever childlike, and want to stay there in regards to those things. I am not supposed to deduct its delicacies and makeup. I am but to worship the One who created them all, and that I joyfully do at any opportunity allotted me, whether in the forest overlooking Bass Lake or in a building worshiping with other believers and a worship team. I do not want to ever lose that wonder.

Let's get back to the wonder of transformation. The word *transformation* has been a Christian catchword for some fifteen years or so. The first time I ever heard of the word *transformation* was in the '90s when I was privileged to be on the ministry team for Dr. C. Peter Wagner for the Prayer and Spiritual Warfare conferences across the United States. It was Ed Silvoso, an Argentinian, who taught and imparted the reality that Jehovah wanted to transform cities and nations. What a concept, how incredible. How could this happen? It seemed impossible considering the condition of our churches, let alone our cities and nations. Amazingly enough a man named George Otis Jr., the son of one of our nation's amazing ministers, answered the call to go to places on this planet and record and dialogue with people in regions where transformation was happening. George wrote *The Last of the Giants*[1] and served as a senior associate with the Lausanne Committee for World Evangelization and coordinator for United Prayer Track for the AD2000 & Beyond Movement. He is a founding director of the World Prayer Center in Colorado Springs, Colorado, and is president of The Sentinel Group, a Christian research and information agency. Wow! When the first Transformation video from The Sentinel Group was released, it brought truth to the statement that one picture is worth a thousand words. We saw how a city in Central America was totally transformed by the power of God through intercession and dealing with the spiritual strongholds of that city.

I was privileged some years after that to lead a team on a prayer journey to Scotland and England. Part of the trip we went to the New Hebrides Islands, where we met with Donald John, the last survivor of the revival that had taken place there many years before. It was an incredible experience being with Donald John and the saints on the island. They were still walking in the throes and residue from that overwhelming revival. It had been over fifty years and still it was evident in the land and in the people. Their prayers and intercession put us to shame. I said to the team, and myself, "We do not know how to pray." There was an anointing like no other I have ever seen or experienced resident in these people. They are simple people who love Jehovah and have received impartations generation to generation that open the heavens, and the ear of the Father is attuned to their prayers.

And that was just one location where transformation has happened and was sustained.

It is no different with man. We are a conglomerate of issues, family generational sin patterns, our own sin choices, our nationality, and on and on. We live in a sin sick world, and our father and mother, Adam and Eve, opened a door that all of us would have walked through. We are left with the need for transformation until we all come to the full knowledge and revelation and transformation of Jesus Christ and His Spirit.

So this transformation process covers everything from A to Z, but the Alpha and the Omega has promised to bring us through that process to the place where we really do look like Him. And just like Apostle Peter, we can be the child of the Father of all things and bring Him great glory and honor, as we carry His DNA into all eternity. We are not like those before the Flood that did not have the opportunity to get it together and make right choices to walk in the image of God. But the Father of us all decided, because of His love, that He would make a way and would bring us all the opportunity of a lifetime (no pun intended) to do it right and see our lives transformed, as well as our cities and nations. Jesus came and brought transformation with a capital T.

I believe this passage shows us that in a short period of time, Jesus's heart for each and every one of us, in spite of our deficiencies. He blesses us with supernatural experiences to open our spiritual eyes, even when we do not get it, and graces us in the midst of our blunders. That is nothing to Him. As He dialogued with Peter, James, and John, they were being transformed and they did not even realize it. They stepped into the realm of the spirit with natural eyes and experienced the kingdom of God on earth.

> Six days later Jesus took Peter and the two brothers, James and John, and led them up a high mountain to be alone. As the men watched, Jesus' appearance was transformed so that his face shone like the sun, and his clothes became as white as light. Suddenly, Moses and Elijah appeared and began talking with Jesus.

Peter blurted out, "Lord, it's wonderful for us to be here! If you want, I'll make three shelters as memorials—one for you, one for Moses, and one for Elijah." But even as he spoke, a bright cloud came over them, and a voice from the cloud said, "This is my dearly loved Son, who brings me great joy. Listen to him." The disciples were terrified and fell face down on the ground. Then Jesus came over and touched them. "Get up," he said. "Don't be afraid." And when they looked, they saw only Jesus. As they went back down the mountain, Jesus commanded them, "Don't tell anyone what you have seen until the Son of Man has been raised from the dead."

—Matthew 17:1–9, NLT

OK, so what's up, Jesus? I have to just laugh here, and so should you. In the midst of an absolutely incredible miracle transferred from heaven to earth, where the presence of God had to be so strong you could hardly stand, sweet, childlike Peter asks to make three huts that would eventually crumble with time to remember this experience. Or possibly he thought they needed a place to sit down and rest from their long trip from the heavenly realm! Even Father Jehovah continues to speak to all in that cloud, and reminds them that this is His Son, and that they should listen to Him. It is stated that they all were terrified and either were slain in the Spirit or just in fear fell down on the ground. Jesus had to come and say, "Get up. Do not be afraid, because I am here to show you the way of the Spirit and show you the way of transformation, and to help you press forward in your own personal destiny."

I just wonder if that was such a defining point for Peter.

He received a huge dose of transformation personally that thrust him forward into that next place he needed to be to become the great Apostle Peter, the rock. He continued to have "foot-in-mouth disease," and I am so glad because I have the same problem. I can fall back on his condition to help me not give up every time I must remove my foot from my mouth due to my condition.

One of the keys of my personal spiritual DNA is truth. It is so important to me to give truth, receive truth, and make sure it is truth. I sometimes, though, give too much information about a certain subject because I want to make sure you understand truth. So if I give you too much information, just move forward to where there is new subject matter within the theme. Be like Jesus and just bless me and move forward knowing there must be some more great information in this book that you can apply to your journey.

This book has taken such a long time to write, and I believe Jehovah needed me to walk through an extensive season of my own destiny to be able to put in print what you needed, to encourage you, and take you to a place where you want to be more than the place you are right now.

> On the way, Jesus told them, "Tonight all of you will desert me. For the Scriptures say, 'God will strike the Shepherd, and the sheep of the flock will be scattered.' But after I have been raised from the dead, I will go ahead of you to Galilee and meet you there." Peter declared, "Even if everyone else deserts you, I will never desert you." Jesus replied, "I tell you the truth, Peter— this very night, before the rooster crows, you will deny three times that you even know me."

> "No!" Peter insisted. "Even if I have to die with
> you, I will never deny you!" And all the other
> disciples vowed the same.
> —Matthew 26:31–35, nlt

This is the beginning of the passages that prompted me to write this book, and even now I weep, because Jesus revealed to me Peter's heart in this shift of his life. Probably—no not probably, for sure—the defining moment comes when Peter realizes who he is and who Jesus is, but it comes through the most painful experience in Peter's life.

Peter and the other disciples are again sitting with Jesus, learning, listening, eating, and drinking. They are also waiting to see Messiah take His place over the Roman government to rule everything, and change things there in that region. Not! Jesus knows what is around the corner, and He is desiring to release truth and prophecy yet to be fulfilled according to His Father's direction. He knows man's heart well and knows how he will respond no matter what His words. Jesus tells them that all will desert Him; in fact, all the disciples will scatter, and so it must be. But precious Peter in childlike faith says, "No way, Jose, it ain't gonna happen. Even if everyone else abandons you, I won't." He is so like us, not knowing what new encounter was waiting around the corner. I am convinced for sure you will be victorious in your position as one of His favorite disciples.

The disciples all stand together in their position that they will never abandon Jesus. But interesting for sure, Jesus turns to Peter only and says with a state of strong emphasis, "Pete, before that chicken crows tonight you will not only abandon Me, but you will curse and say you do not even know Me." Ouch! Sorry folks, but sometimes it really hurts when we find out how weak, fearful, and so human we are. It is only in His power, and by His Spirit, that we can do anything whatsoever. Get over yourself; it is only in Him that we live. Only He can make the way into our destiny passable. We must choose to submit to it and go through every gate, every doorway, every relationship, every pain that makes it feel like your life is ebbing away, every failure (all of which are seedbeds of success) and rejection.

There will always be a process required to become His disciple, a little Christ. Truly we are destined to be just that very thing. If we can only get it and see that as we lay down our lives daily we will see that fullness manifested, and our destiny carry us down the mountain into the arms of our Lover, our Lord. We will cross the finish line; we will see His face and His reward even here in many ways. Yes, there are many more rewards eternally, but there are rewards here on earth also. Great time to recommend keeping a record of all He does in, through, for you on this journey.

Chapter 8

"THIS REALLY IS THE MESSIAH AND I REALLY AM HIS DISCIPLE"

*A*T THIS JUNCTURE in Peter's conversion to becoming Petra the rock, things are starting to look up. Like Peter, we have to walk through a lot of life—at least I have. The older I get, the more I realize that life itself is a major tool Father uses to take us from glory to glory, level to level, and destiny to greater destiny. As we walk daily through life, we realize that we have not given up; we have made it through sufficient trials and testings to see that truly Jesus has walked with us all along the way. You might think this strange because it seems more like this is the worst place possible in Peter's life; but once you get to the other side and look back, it is clearly visible that this is the defining moment of Peter's life. This is that place where he meets himself face-to-face, and recalls his very words, "I will never leave you, I will die for you."

> Meanwhile, Peter was sitting outside in the court-yard. A servant girl came over and said to him, "You were one of those with Jesus the Galilean." But Peter denied it in front of everyone. "I don't know what you're talking about," he said. Later, out by the gate, another servant girl noticed him

and said to those standing around, "This man was with Jesus of Nazareth." Again Peter denied it, this time with an oath. "I don't even know the man," he said. A little later some of the other bystanders came over to Peter and said, "You must be one of them; we can tell by your Galilean accent." Peter swore, "A curse on me if I'm lying—I don't know the man!" And immediately the rooster crowed. Suddenly, Jesus' words flashed through Peter's mind: "Before the rooster crows, you will deny three times that you even know me." And he went away, weeping bitterly.

—MATTHEW 26:69–75, NLT

Jesus doesn't enable us by getting us out of every fix we get ourselves entangled in. He is truly there, cheering us on and telling us we can make it. He realizes "Jacob's limp" in Peter. He knows Peter will prevail and make it through to that place of glory in Christ, after the Resurrection and after the Day of Pentecost. In this place, Peter has been humbled to such a degree that the humiliation and pain he experiences is the very thing that allows him to press on to the high calling he now knows he has been called to.

Peter stands, totally naked emotionally, totally in confusion. This is just not working out like he thought it would. Where is the takeover of the government? Where are the thrones next to Jesus in glory? Where is the position Peter thought was going to be his own? No, this is the worst of the worst, the place of pain so excruciating that the mind just cannot function properly. This is that place that every person called to greatness in Jehovah's kingdom must traverse. A meeting of the minds, yours and His, you could say; a place where truth slaps you in the face and you must face your worst introduction to who you really are, frail human being, not able to accomplish anything, not able to stand the pressure of trails and tests, ready to chuck it all and just go hide in a cave for the rest of your life. So real, so true, and so necessary.

This is the place where Jehovah revealed to me Peter's heart there in the midst of that courtyard, out in the open. Why was he there? Had he been following the guards who took Jesus from the garden? Had he walked close by, or was he walking at a distance? What was he thinking—if he even could think—considering what had just transpired? Remember he had lopped off the ear of one of the guards, which certainly would have been a bloody mess. Even in the midst of that, Jesus calmly reaches down, retrieves the ear, and miraculously reattaches it to the guard's head.

We know by the report in Scripture that there was an intrusion of the power of God that impacted every person standing there. Even in the midst of a bloody chaotic situation, destiny was being stretched forward into the place where Peter would become all Jesus had said He would become. Later on, adding insult to injury and even more stress to this hellish nightmare, a man declares again that Peter had been with Jesus. And in fact, the man was the relative of the man who temporarily lost the ear, and he recognized who Peter was.

> But one of the household slaves of the high priest, a relative of the man whose ear Peter had cut off, asked, "Didn't I see you out there in the olive grove with Jesus?" Again Peter denied it. And immediately a rooster crowed.
> —JOHN 18:26–27, NLT

It is in this place that Peter faces his worst fear; everything he thought Jesus was and would do was imploding right before his eyes. But he could not leave the scene, and followed the trail of people to Caiaphas's house, where Jesus would be tried. All this time his thoughts went back and forth, and his heart prepared to break open in regret, fear, and even terror; the possibility of losing his own life was right in his face, but still he couldn't leave. He had to carry this out to the end no matter what; he had to know what was happening.

Did he remember Jesus talking to him and the other disciples of what was coming and how it would be, and what they must do? Were they just empty words on empty ears? So like us; we hear truth in no uncertain terms, but until it is tested, we rarely really believe it.

This is the place where the double-edged sword of the kingdom must be put into your hands. Every person must come to this place of realizing the double-edged sword, which is a good thing, but needs understanding and experience to wield. This sword is on one hand the reality that we are but grass, red dirt; organic material that by itself is just that; inert components, molded into a man; but nothing yet, until the Creator breathes His life into us and plants within man a spirit, which will live forever.

You must understand that the flesh realizes it has an end, that it will at some point no longer be able to rise up trying to control our lives. So with that being understood, realize the flesh will do absolutely anything to use the time it has to bask in desire, not caring what it does mentally, physically, or spiritually. Its only desire is to fulfill the lusty pleasures of this world system and the kingdom of darkness. It will destroy itself if it can. It must be kept under self-control, which Galatians tells us is one of the fruits of the Spirit (Gal. 5:22–23).

The other side of this double-edged sword is the reality that we were formed by the hand of the Creator of the universe—unique, special, and one of a kind. Psalm 139 makes that very clear:

> O Lord, you have examined my heart and know everything about me. You know when I sit down or stand up. You know my thoughts even when I'm far away. You see me when I travel and when I rest at home. You know everything I do. You know what I am going to say even before I say it, Lord. You go before me and follow me. You place your hand of blessing on my head. Such knowledge is too wonderful for me, too great for me to understand! I can never escape from your Spirit! I can never get away from your presence! If I go up to heaven, you are there; if I go down to the grave, you are there. If I ride the wings of the morning, if I dwell by the farthest oceans, even there your hand will guide me, and your strength will support me. I could ask the darkness to hide me and the light around me to become night—but even in darkness I cannot hide from you. To you the night shines as bright as day. Darkness and light are the same to you.
>
> *You made all the delicate, inner parts of my body and knit me together in my mother's womb. Thank you for making me so wonderfully complex! Your workmanship is marvelous— how well I know it. You watched me as I was being formed in utter seclusion, as I was woven*

together in the dark of the womb. You saw me before I was born. Every day of my life was recorded in your book. Every moment was laid out before a single day had passed. How precious are your thoughts about me, O God. They cannot be numbered! I can't even count them; they outnumber the grains of sand! And when I wake up, you are still with me!
—Psalm 139:1–18, nlt, emphasis added

He destined us for greatness, each and every one. But you must understand His perspective of greatness, and this is not as our world system presents. It is a greater greatness as a son or daughter of God than we believe. The liar has worked diligently at keeping it away from us and using every method in his arsenal to steal, kill, and destroy us and our destiny purpose. It is time to take back our lives and our destiny and leave behind the rubbish and every evil thing that has pushed itself into our being, families, generations, and nations.

I must remind you that you have been bought with a price. Your life is not your own; it belongs to Him who created and formed you, and watched you being brought forth into this sin-sick system to be His child, His instrument of joy, peace, love, power, and authority, and to take His kingdom back to Him.

The blood of Jesus is quite a price to pay to get back what belonged to you in the first place; it is truly beyond anything you or I can conceive of or fully understand. We stand speechless before this. There is nothing to say but yes, a resounding yes, to the destiny that was prepared for us before the foundations of the world were even conceived.

This other side of the sword is a kingly place, an

inheritance we do not deserve or even have to lift a finger to bring forth. It has been given freely, as we have freely accepted His grace to save, seal, and deliver us from this thing that doesn't even deserve to be named, to bring us back to what was written in our books of life, and our destiny that is reverberating in the heavenly realm.

If we could see those books, I believe we would all be astounded at their contents. We have on this side of the sword all that is needed to complete our destiny purpose, all that will take us from glory to glory and to the fulfillment of our individual destinies, as well as Father's purpose for this planet and His kingdom.

Do not be dismayed at what you see with the natural eye; see it as an opportunity to bring forth His divine purpose and plan, declared by His very mouth in His written Word to us. It is time for us to begin to really believe this book written so long ago that has stayed the centuries of time and not been lost or stolen or forgotten. It is strong, it is alive, and it will not fail.

I pray that you will also have come to that place and realize this very thing in your own life. It truly is a day of new beginnings in new levels, and we are all going to make it up this mountain. We will see Him face-to-face, and we will hear those beautiful greetings when we see Him.

Our precious Peter is now pressed full force into this place, and in a short period of time his heart has ruptured into many pieces. He realizes what he has done of his own free will.

He has come face-to-face with himself; everything that has taken place in the last few hours runs like a video across his mind, and he is a broken man. It is from this place of brokenness that he takes a giant step into a new place where he will receive on the day of Pentecost the power and indwelling of Holy Spirit to take him higher and higher. It certainly doesn't look like it at this hellish place, but it is nonetheless. He will never forget this day, never forget what he did, but he will know at levels he never knew before the power of forgiveness of self and sin to that place of victory over every assault and choice he has made. It is a new day.

THINK ABOUT IT

1. So, it's time to evaluate where you are and where you want to be in the next six months or so.

2. Are you ready—of course not—for the coming days? In prayer and supplication, make your requests known to your heavenly Father and He will answer and keep you as He promised.

3. This is a good time to be real with yourself and accept the fact that it is OK. You have come to where every other human has come; some succeeded, and some failed because they did not choose Jesus.

4. This could be your defining moment. Write about it to yourself.

Chapter 9

THE PEBBLE IS NOW BEING FORGED IN THE ROCK

Matthew 26:58; Mark 14:54

*I*T IS EASY for us to read these passages in the Bible and say, "Wow, I could never be like that," and put Peter up on a pedestal. Peter would never want to be put on a pedestal, and we must see clearly through the Gospels, the Book of Acts, and the Epistles, that Peter's humility came with a huge price tag; it came from being challenged again and again by Jesus and circumstances, in the midst of his humanity. He did persevere and so must we. We too are being forged into rocks of righteousness and power that are being placed as part of the foundation, where Jesus is the Cornerstone.

THE DARK NIGHT OF THE SOUL

Scripture gives us a clear picture of what took place during this terrible time for all the disciples. Their world was being ripped apart, and this One, the Messiah, was just not doing what they thought He was going to do and should do. Yes, He had told them repeatedly that this would happen just as it did; but their mind-sets would not let them see the reality

71

of the Cross, or the characteristic of humility as a powerful weapon to overcome all things. They did not see His willingness to give us His human life willingly and so painfully for their and our sake.

He was supposed to be a mighty leader, a king who would take over the Roman government and take control of these people. He was supposed to set up a worldly kingdom where they could all be in positions over people and be really popular, or at least wealthy and of high society. Oh, so much like us. We will all cross this bed of red-hot coals to find that none of this was ever true, nor would we even want it to be true.

Many have stated remarks about "the dark night of the soul," and they are always negative. I wish to add to it a positive. This is probably one of the best places where heaven invades earth in humanity and brings a force beyond anything we can conceive. We are certainly in a vulnerable position, a place where our flesh is certainly beaten to a pulp and doesn't have much strength at the moment. It is a crucible from which each one must drink—and drink it all—in order for the medicine to go down (and there is no spoon of sugar to help it). Down it must go. It tastes terrible, but once it is down it can begin to work through the intricate places of body, soul, and spirit; especially the mind, breaking down the structure we have erected out of our own ability.

The old Erector Sets were so incredible—so many pieces, so looking like nothing in its initial state when you opened the box. But by following the instructions, and using the tools that are included, incredible skyscrapers could be erected and enjoyed. And they were not like legos or building blocks that could so easily crumble at the slightest nudge. Our lives must be built on Christ the Rock, or we will topple and fall. We must be taken through that desert of death to self so that we can have new eyes to see, and a transformed mind to receive heavenly revelation.

Each of us is called to be a rock, to be forged in the mighty hand of Jehovah, Yahweh, Lord of the universe, any of hundreds of names that represent Him, to be His instrument of His design, of His plan, of His way and not our own.

We all start out with grandiose ideas of what we can do, great educations, great families, great whatever. But that all will crumble and we must come back to square one: Jehovah, Yeshua, and Holy Spirit. That's it. They are the One and Ones who must have first priority in our lives. We have tons of scriptures that state that clearly. Just open your Bible anywhere and I am sure you will find an appropriate scripture to confirm this. Along with those passages are the hundreds of incredible promises available to us as we lay down our lives, die, and are raised to life in the Spirit of God.

What is so awesome is that the dark night of the soul is but a season; it is not permanent, no matter what the devil tells you. Everything is seasonal; it is a basic principle of the kingdom as well as nature itself. There is an end and there is new life out of the dregs of death; and there is a future, a destiny that has been forged in you for your good as well as the Father's. You do come through that desert place to a place of beauty; a field of beautiful wildflowers with such a pungent sweet fragrance that it overwhelms you, and you feel as if you are floating across that field.

Make your way to that place and stretch your life forward as a runner presses onward to the finish line. It is always there before you. Until you run through the tape at the end of the race, the finish line will always be right in front of you, waiting for you to break its taut stretch across the track. It yearns for you to break it, to make it fall to the ground. It brings you that rush of adrenaline right as you cross the line, even though you are out of breath and every muscle in your body is wasted from the race; but you are done, finished, *finito*, passed the test, made it, and you are the victor.

Take joy in knowing you were worth all you went through. He called you by name. He chose you for this destiny. He didn't just make you part of a list of folks that might make it. You were the only name on this list. Each person's name is the only one on the list. You were hand-selected for this destiny and it is guaranteed. The only cost to you is saying yes. The cost to the heavenly Father was great: the life of His only Son, the incarnate God of the universe. This should make us want to run that race even harder than before.

Just to make sure you realize, I have not arrived, I have not pressed through that finish line tape. I am still in process, my destiny is not complete, but I am pressing onward—don't stumble as much as I used to, got the scars to prove it. I am determined to walk this out. This is the reason I wrote this book. It was made clear to me that the body of Christ needed this book for these days. I want to get the message to as many sisters and brothers as possible.

I was and still am an only child in my family. When I came into the kingdom and became a part of the family of God, I took on all of you as the siblings I never had, So like it or not, I am here for the duration—yes, eternity—and we have to get together and believe for one another, encourage one another, and help one another across that finish line. Hebrews makes it very clear; the great cloud of witnesses is waiting for us to finish the race. It clearly states that until we finish our race, they cannot receive their reward. The patriarchs of old—Moses, Daniel, Rebecca, Jacob, Matthew, Mark, Luke, and John, and on and on—they are waiting for us to complete our destiny, as they completed theirs, so we can all together receive our reward. They know we are just like them, with all our stuff. They know our struggles, for you see, they struggled too. And for all of time, all their failures recorded are there to teach us that we too can make it, that we are destined for greatness as they were. And there are so many we do not even know about.

This is such an incredible life we have been given. We will one day stand at the throne of the one and only living God and say, "Now I see it fully." But until then, let's keep moving forward into our personal destiny and training with new strength and new revelation.

Time to Pause

1. Reward yourself for coming this far.

2. Do your own timeline up to this point and stand back and be amazed. Be creative, maybe even have it framed!

Chapter 10

BEING BURIED WITH JESUS

"Now go and tell his disciples, including Peter, that Jesus is going ahead of you to Galilee. You will see him there, just as he told you before he died." The women fled from the tomb, trembling and bewildered, and they said nothing to anyone because they were too frightened.

[MARK 16:7–8, NLT]

Still later he appeared to the eleven disciples as they were eating together. He rebuked them for their stubborn unbelief because they refused to believe those who had seen him after he had been raised from the dead. And then he told them, "Go into all the world and preach the Good News to everyone. Anyone who believes and is baptized will be saved. But anyone who refuses to believe will be condemned. These miraculous signs will accompany those who believe: They will cast out demons in my name, and they will speak in new languages. They will be able to handle snakes with safety, and if they drink anything poisonous, it won't hurt them. They will be able to place their hands on the sick, and they will be healed."

[MARK 16:14–18, NLT]

$\mathcal{I}$T'S RESURRECTION DAY, and the women who encounter the risen Christ are speechless and terrified. They have encountered Jesus on His way to find His disciples. He talked with them as well as many others before His final departure back to heaven, where He sits at the right hand of the Father interceding on our behalf. And what are the first words out of His mouth? "Tell Peter and the others." Jesus knows full well what Peter has just gone through. In fact, in the midst of His dying a horrendous death, after the mutilation of His body, going to get the keys of hell and death, and then coming back to the earth realm he had just left, He speaks for all of time the words, "Tell Peter." While in the midst of all He was doing, Jesus saw Peter's agony, saw his broken and ravaged heart, and saw the confusion, the questions, and the pain.

He wants the women there to make sure Peter knows, "I'm back." His great pebble, in Peter's eyes, His disciple, has need of encouragement, needs to know his Redeemer lives and that all is well. You might even want to look at Peter's three days as a small typology of Jesus's experience the past three days. "Peter, precious Peter, it's OK. I'm here and everything will happen just as I told you." We are not told Peter's response when the women found him and relayed the message from Jesus, but you know and I know it was an eye opener. It got his attention right away, whether he let anyone know or not. His mind had to be reeling over what had been reported to him.

I really don't think Peter was thinking theologically about all Jesus said, about him misunderstanding absolutely everything. I believe his heart leapt in his chest, and there was warm oil poured out on Peter from the top of his head to the bottom of his feet. His eternal damnation of himself has turned to joy in his risen Redeemer, Restorer of all the past, all the words, all the thoughts, all the presumption of the past three years. It is a new beginning for Peter and for all of humanity from that point forward, even to us today and beyond to those yet born. His "hoof-in-mouth disease" has just been healed forever.

And then a few miles down the road in verses 14–18, Jesus hooks up with his "homies." What a glorious day. All the questions that were bottled up in his heart and mind, all the shock of everything that has taken place in the last three days, and now this beautiful joy mixed with more emotions and thoughts have taken hold of Peter, disciple of the risen Messiah.

The first thing Jesus does when He encounters the disciples is rebuke their unbelief. He is on a fast track to heaven and He can't mince any words. These are His chosen ones, His apostles of the early church. They must have a three-day seminar shrunken into one hour, one-on-one intervention, if you like, addressing what needs to be said so they can move forward into birthing the church of Jesus Christ. This is so indicative of intimate relationship with Jesus. He was not there judging them. He was discipling them.

They were together for those three years in incredible times of life, ministry, and building personal relationships with one another and with Jesus. They experienced the teaching to the multitudes, which was also for them. He taught them things He did not teach the multitudes. They watched as He healed the sick and raised the dead to life right in front of their eyes. They were the first ones to be released into ministry with the anointing of Jesus to also heal the sick and raise the dead, cast out demons, and make more disciples. They ate together, lived together, and walked dusty roads all across the holy land, from city to city. They watched history being written in each experience. They would later relate those experiences by the anointing and power of Holy Spirit in written form for you and me to receive for the same purpose.

They had to know Him in ways no one else did, so that they could continue their destiny call. They would lay the foundations on which we stand today by the power of that same Holy Spirit.

He knows that they must take the next step and be buried with Him in their unbelief and stubbornness. Remember, Jesus knows that in a short period of time He is going to send to them Holy Spirit as their Comforter to be with them 24/7 from now on. So they must deal with this unbelief and stubbornness first. This is so true for us also. The enemy of our souls will use unbelief to take us out. We live in a world of unbelief, in spite of what is before our very eyes. Unbelief is a cancer and will destroy your faith if you allow it.

Jesus keeps the main thing the main thing: Repent of this unbelief right now before we go any further. Let it drop to the ground and crush it under your feet.

I would highly suggest we do the same. It is always creeping around any corner, ready to grab us in the midst of a difficult situation or circumstance. It is not only unbelief, He says, but "stubborn unbelief." He nailed them, and it is clear as history shows that from this day forward unbelief never touched them again, especially Peter. Just look at his message on the Day of Pentecost. Wow, go Peter.

Front correction to commissioning in one breath. How awesome. From this juncture Jesus then prophesies over them and over all peoples upon the earth the greatest job assignment ever. It is the mandate of heaven, the Father's destiny for every individual who will follow hard after Jesus and His kingdom. He declares and imparts to them the awesome responsibility, as well as anointing, to first go into the entire world. No holds barred, no limitations; all the nations of the earth, no excuses.

Jesus declares six statements. One for each day of the week, minus Sabbath! He does this all in one breath. He knows they have dealt with their stubborn unbelief, and now He releases them to the rock level of ministry for the kingdom of the Father.

1. Go

2. Tell everyone the good news of salvation

3. Miraculous signs will follow all who believe (not just the original apostles)

4. You will cast out demons

5. Speak in new languages

6. Heal the sick

> When the Lord Jesus had finished talking with them, he was taken up into heaven and sat down in the place of honor at God's right hand. And the disciples went everywhere and preached, and the Lord worked through them, confirming what they said by many miraculous signs.
>
> —MARK 16:19–20, NLT

Immediately following Jesus's conversation with Peter and the disciples, He was taken up into heaven. The Scriptures in themselves make a huge statement in the writing, because the segue from correction to commissioning to doing is instant. Nothing else needed to be said. They knew at that moment they had stepped through a veil of destiny that they were finally able to grasp and step into. They also knew they would never go back the same way they had previously come. They were setting their foreheads like flint and forward was the only gear in their vehicle. No turning back. They had been buried with Jesus, and they now were resurrected to a new life, an abundant life; a life filled with love, grace, power, and anointing that would forever change the world.

This very same gift, if you would like to call it that, is yours. It really is more than a gift. It is an enablement of supernatural means beyond anything you or I could ever conjure up or even come to any mental assent. It is of the heavenly realm of the kingdom of Jehovah; His Son, Jesus the Christ; and Holy Spirit, the Comforter, Teacher, and more. You stand at that very same place, and you too must receive, by choice, to take the same steps that Peter and his friends did. It is on your plate now. It is awesome, I promise. Go for it.

TIME TO PAUSE

1. You should be ready to take another step. Lay it out as Holy Spirit directs you. It will be different for everyone.

2. Seek wise counselors and those that will encourage you on your path of destiny. Be accountable for it.

3. I made myself accountable to complete this manuscript, and had to discipline myself strongly to complete it. So discipline yourself to not give up, moving in forward all the time.

Chapter 11

LIFE AFTER RESURRECTION AND BEING A HOME BOY AGAIN

Acts 1:13

When they arrived, they went to the upstairs room of the house where they were staying. Here are the names of those who were present: Peter, John, James, Andrew, Philip, Thomas, Bartholomew, Matthew, James (son of Alphaeus), Simon (the Zealot), and Judas (son of James). They all met together and were constantly united in prayer, along with Mary the mother of Jesus, several other women, and the brothers of Jesus. During this time, when about 120 believers were together in one place, Peter stood up and addressed them. "Brothers," he said, "the Scriptures had to be fulfilled concerning Judas, who guided those who arrested Jesus. This was predicted long ago by the Holy Spirit, speaking through King David. Judas was one of us and shared in the ministry with us." (Judas had bought a field with the money he received for his treachery. Falling headfirst there, his body split open, spilling out all his intestines. The news of his death spread to all the people of Jerusalem, and they gave the place the Aramaic name *Akeldama*, which means "Field of Blood.")

Peter continued, "This was written in the book of Psalms, where it says, 'Let his home become desolate, with no one living in it.' It also says, 'Let someone else take his position.' "So now we must choose a replacement for Judas from among the men who were with us the entire time we were traveling with the Lord Jesus—from the time he was baptized by John until the day he was taken from us. Whoever is chosen will join us as a witness of Jesus' resurrection." So they nominated two men: Joseph called Barsabbas (also known as Justus) and Matthias. Then they all prayed, "O Lord, you know every heart. Show us which of these men you have chosen as an apostle to replace Judas in this ministry, for he has deserted us and gone where he belongs." Then they cast lots, and Matthias was selected to become an apostle with the other eleven.

[ACTS 1:13–26, NLT]

*T*HIS CURRENT CHAPTER in this book and in Peter's life is a whole new thing. No more Peter the pebble. The rock has emerged, so put your seatbelt on and get ready for a roller coaster ride of epic proportions.

First thing they have all gathered in that Upper Room. They have come to wait as Jesus told them to do. Peter steps up to the plate with faith, hope, and authority. He addresses each one of them as brothers as they are gathered there. He begins right off declaring what everybody was talking about in whispers around the room. What about Judas? What happened? Why? Why didn't Jesus do something about His betrayal?

What the majority did not know was that Jesus had spoken clearly that evening when He and the disciples sat around the table having their traditional Jewish Passover dinner. He said clearly that one of them would betray Him, and even told Judas face-to-face to go quickly and do what was in his heart to do. I am sure Peter remembers that, but there is no need to address that information at this time. He immediately goes to King David's writings and shares with them the prophecies declaring about Judas and what he would do in betraying the Messiah. Peter's authority as the rock has been established in this 120-person church of Jesus Christ now forming. He declares that this had to happen, and shares with all the exact gory details of Judas's death. He knows by the Spirit, even though the Spirit has yet to be poured out on all, that the order of the government of Messiah must be put back intact, so he declares that they must choose a replacement for Judas. The person must be a firsthand witness of Jesus's resurrection. Matthias is chosen by prayer and a throwing of the lot, used to determine the will of the Father.

Peter stands confident before the 120. There are no accusations against what he had done in the garden and the courtyard. I do not think it left Peter's memory, but was a beautiful reminder and a testimony of what Jesus will do with a broken heart and broken life surrendered to him, no matter what the circumstances are at the time. Peter stands tall, prophesying and declaring, and also establishing himself as a major leader among the apostles now guiding the baby church of Jesus Christ.

Peter has come through the birth canal. He has come into a new revelation and relationship with the Messiah. He has taken his place and become the rock on which Jesus would build his church, just as Jesus had spoken to him when he was but a mouthy, small pebble in everyone's eyes.

We too must come the very same way. Different circumstances, different time, but we all must come through that place that desires to take our lives and sanity. But Jesus proved that He would make a way. He promised He would wipe away every tear and every sorrow so we could and would become a rock for His purposes. He set us up to establish His kingdom on earth, to take back what the enemy had stolen and bring it to the feet of Jesus, that He would give it to His Father, Jehovah.

Where are you today? Where are you in the process? What is hampering you from moving over that mountain of excuses and circumstances? It really is only you and your stubborn unbelief. Remember what Jesus told the people. It only takes the faith of a mustard seed to speak to any mountain, any circumstance, and tell it to crumble. What's keeping the tiny seed from sprouting in your hand right now? *Nothing!* So move forward. You're about to take off at breaking speed and feel the wind of the Spirit of God on your face. You're going to soar over everything, and you're going to take dominion over all that Jehovah has placed in your destiny for His purposes.

Chapter 12

THE ROCK

Acts 2:14-41

Peter Preaches to the Crowd

Then Peter stepped forward with the eleven other apostles and shouted to the crowd, "Listen carefully, all of you, fellow Jews and residents of Jerusalem! Make no mistake about this. These people are not drunk, as some of you are assuming. Nine o'clock in the morning is much too early for that. No, what you see was predicted long ago by the prophet Joel: 'In the last days,' God says, 'I will pour out my Spirit upon all people. Your sons and daughters will prophesy. Your young men will see visions, and your old men will dream dreams. In those days I will pour out my Spirit even on my servants—men and women alike—and they will prophesy. And I will cause wonders in the heavens above and signs on the earth below—blood and fire and clouds of smoke. The sun will become dark, and the moon will turn blood red before that great and glorious day of the LORD arrives. But everyone who calls on the name of the LORD will be saved.' "People of Israel, listen! God publicly endorsed Jesus the Nazarene by doing powerful miracles, wonders, and signs through him, as you well know. But God knew what would happen, and his prearranged plan was carried out when Jesus was betrayed. With the help of lawless Gentiles, you nailed him to a cross and killed him. But God released him from the horrors of death and raised him back to life, for death could not keep him in its grip. King David said this about him: 'I see that the LORD is always with me. I will not be shaken, for he is right beside me. No wonder my heart is glad, and my tongue shouts his praises! My body rests in hope. For you will not leave my soul among the dead or allow your Holy One to rot in the grave. You have shown me the way of life, and you will fill me with the joy of your presence.'

"Dear brothers, think about this! You can be sure that the patriarch David wasn't referring to himself, for he died and was buried, and his tomb is still here among us. But he was a prophet, and he knew God had promised with an oath that one of David's own descendants would sit on his throne. David was looking into the future and speaking of the Messiah's resurrection. He was saying that God would not leave him among the dead or allow his body to rot in the grave. God raised Jesus from the dead, and we are all witnesses of this. Now he is exalted to the place of highest honor in heaven, at God's right hand. And the Father, as he had promised, gave him the Holy Spirit to pour out upon us, just as you see and hear today. For David himself never ascended into heaven, yet he said, 'The LORD said to my Lord, "Sit in the place of honor at my right hand until I humble your enemies, making them a footstool under your feet."' So let everyone in Israel know for certain that God has made this Jesus, whom you crucified, to be both Lord and Messiah!" Peter's words pierced their hearts, and they said to him and to the other apostles, "Brothers, what should we do?" Peter replied, "Each of you must repent of your sins, turn to God, and be baptized in the name of Jesus Christ to show that you have received forgiveness for your sins. Then you will receive the gift of the Holy Spirit. This promise is to you, and to your children, and even to the Gentiles—all who have been called by the Lord our God." Then Peter continued preaching for a long time, strongly urging all his listeners, "Save yourselves from this crooked generation!" Those who believed what Peter said were baptized and added to the church that day—about 3,000 in all.

[Acts 2:14–41, nlt]

*T*HIS IS ONE of the most powerful sermons ever preached in all of time. The mighty Peter the Apostle begins to speak under the power of the Spirit of God; all that the enemy has thrown at him is now dirt under his feet. He has within him the faith of the ages ready to release the kingdom of God upon the people there waiting in that surreal place for the outpouring of the Holy Spirit upon all mankind. It had to start somewhere, and this was the place to be.

Peter's words were of the ages past, but were like a mighty wind that thrust forth across those hearing. They were words of prophecy spoken many years before, and now were being manifested in their very presence. Here was Peter, the simple fisherman, loudly and with great authority proclaiming the risen Savior, the Son of the living God. The anointing was so strong on him that three thousand were added to the blossoming church of Jesus Christ that one day—not even really one full day, but as the result of one message spoken by Peter the Apostle.

He makes it clear that it is they who put Jesus to death. And clearly he knows he was part of that death sentence by his words and actions. But now they no longer have any power over him. He has overcome truly by the blood of the Lamb of God and by his very own testimony. He has proven to himself and all those around that Jesus Christ is the true Messiah, and clearly in Him and Him alone is salvation and eternal life.

Peter has been filled with the power of Holy Spirit. He is under an incredible anointing and begins to testify to all who could hear that they must repent of their sins and be baptized. It is clearly stated that Peter's words pierced their hearts; a multitude were brought to that place to which each of us must come. We must humble ourselves and realize we cannot hold our lives together on our own. We can only do it under the power of Jesus Christ and Holy Spirit. Those in attendance not only believed that Jesus was the Messiah, but they were baptized that very day.

TIME TO PAUSE

1. I want you to make the questions here that you need to answer.

2. You have come this far, and I trust you, like Peter, have something to say, even if only to yourself and Jehovah, Jesus, and Holy Spirit.

Chapter 13

THE COMMISSIONING
AND IN CONCLUSION

*T*HE LORD OF the universe is not looking for people with potential. You are all He has and all He has ever wanted. You were born with potential; you are born with destiny. You cannot get away from it no matter how hard you try. Potential is just an excuse for not paying the price for your destiny. Yes, there is a price you have to pay. I am sure by now you know that quite well, and have already paid part of that tuition, or you would not be reading this book (and especially not to the end).

The destiny of mankind is definitely not for wimps. Even though we may start as a wimp, you have to start somewhere—it is a start. Even believing you can start is great faith, in my estimation. The conclusion to this all is now go forward. Use this as a tool for this season. I am sure there will be more on the way for you. Use it to disciple others. Use your journey and the chronicling you have done in this process to urge them on, undergirding them as you have been undergirded. Be honest with them about your successes and your failures. I promise it will help dissolve their stubborn unbelief.

In John 21, Jesus told Peter three times to feed His

sheep. That same assignment has been given to each one of us, that we might feed others of the same manna we have received. We must go and make disciples of nations, not just a neighbor across the street.

> Those who believed what Peter said were baptized and added to the church that day—about 3,000 in all.
>
> —ACTS 2:41, NLT

THE BELIEVERS FORM A COMMUNITY

> All the believers devoted themselves to the apostles' teaching, and to fellowship, and to sharing in meals (including the Lord's Supper), and to prayer. A deep sense of awe came over them all, and the apostles performed many miraculous signs and wonders. And all the believers met together in one place and shared everything they had. They sold their property and possessions and shared the money with those in need. They worshiped together at the Temple each day, met in homes for the Lord's Supper, and shared their meals with great joy and generosity—all the while praising God and enjoying the goodwill of all the people. And each day the Lord added to their fellowship those who were being saved.
>
> —ACTS 2:42–47, NLT

Can you see the beautiful picture that has been birthed to life after Peter preaches in such power and authority? They became a community, a family, different than ever before. The fruit of all of Peter's destiny pursuit has now become a loaded-down grapevine with huge, sweet clusters of grapes bending the vine to almost breaking due to the weight. We are commanded to bear fruit, much fruit, and fruit that will last. If we do not, we will be severed from the vine, drop to the ground, and be thrown into the burn pile. Here is another piece of truth that I must declare because it is His Word to us.

THE ANOINTING

The anointing is in the cluster. One grape is not going to satisfy anyone, unless you are an ant! We are a team, a living kingdom on earth; you will encounter destiny in yourself and in others every day of your life, if you're willing to open your eyes and see it. You lead the way to become that community, that cluster. You already have a great location: your home. What better place to expand the kingdom of God than in your neighborhood and in your community? Let us together become the fruit of heaven to feed the famished souls of many who cross our paths every day just looking for someone with real food to satisfy their souls.

We see the community of the living organism, the church Jesus told them about, explode into being. And we are told they continued with it. It wasn't just for a short season and then became old hat. It became a lifestyle for the rest of their lives. And so it must be the same for us. The example is beautiful. What an example to the world, and those who have yet believed. I will let the Scriptures speak for themselves, and trust you to implement it within your sphere of influence wherever you live.

From this juncture in the Book of Acts, Peter and the other disciples explode across the known world taking the truth and power of the gospel to all mankind. They bask in the anointing released to them as a graduation present from their heavenly Father and release it to others, even to the point of Peter's shadow bringing healing to a man in need.

They continue to preach the gospel, with boldness and signs and wonders following their preaching. They encounter opposition of every kind, from individuals to government officials. It is a different story now. There is no slipping away in fear from persecution. Peter stands tall and never backs down again, never again to be broken by his stubborn unbelief. He continues for the rest of his life making disciples, healing the sick, raising the dead, casting out demons, and establishing the kingdom of God upon the earth in his generation.

The Lord will always confirm and commission you into your destiny. He did with Peter when He showed him that he was commissioned to take the gospel to the Gentiles. In the past he would have had a fit, but now through multiple ways Peter receives a greater commissioning to take this incredible message to the Gentiles. What an awesome privilege, and we can thank God for that. If Peter had rejected the commissioning, none of us Gentiles might have eternal life. Think about it!

At the juncture decided by Holy Spirit, we know nothing more about Peter. We know he continued to his dying breath living with the passion of the Christ forged in him. He never gave up, never turned back again.

I am thrilled to have been able to see Peter's heart, especially in the worst of times. It has helped me with my own difficult and worst times up to this point in my life. I will look forward to sitting down with Peter one day and discussing with him so much more than I can see and discern. It will be a glorious day.

I trust you are on a greater journey than when you began. If not, I have failed in my endeavor to instruct you and encourage you. I again reiterate as I did back some chapters. Send me your story, your journey, your testimony, so that I might be encouraged, and we might be encouraged together. Then one day in eternity, we too can sit down together and talk about it in realms we didn't know existed.

Your Story

1. You write the questions.

2. You journal the journey.

3. You tell others of the great exploits Jehovah has given you.

4. You make disciples and fulfill the Great Commission. That's what I'm doing!

NOTES

CHAPTER 7

1. George Otis, Jr., *The Last of the Giants* (Grand Rapids: Chosen Books, 1991).

ABOUT THE AUTHOR

*C*ANDI'S PURPOSE IN life is to support you in receiving certainty and truth so that wisdom is imparted, hope and courage arise, and you are free to move forward to fulfill your destiny with integrity and excellence. In 2000 she founded Destiny Training Center in the High Sierras of California, an equipping center raising up the saints for the work of the ministry. In 2009, the High Sierra Epicenter Prayer Room was dedicated. It is an international 24/7 prayer room situated in the geographical heart of California at the southern gate to Yosemite National Park. She and her husband, Don, have lived in the High Sierra mountains for more than twenty-five years. They have two daughters and sons-in-law, and five grandchildren, all following after the heart of Jehovah.

OTHER BOOKS WRITTEN BY THE AUTHOR:

Take Back the Night

CONTACT THE AUTHOR

To contact Dr. Candi MacAlpine for information or
invitations to minister:
e-mail: angel4u@sti.net
website: www.destinytraining.org